CW01394456

A LITTLE BIRD TOLD ME...

by
Philip E. Smith

Published by Sherington Historical Society (www.mkheritage.co.uk/shhs)

With funding from Milton Keynes Heritage Association (www.mkheritage. co.uk)

First published 2013

ISBN: 978-0-9575693-0-0

Front cover illustration by Caroline Leslie

Back cover illustration by Martin Williams

Contents

In the Beginning	1
Schooldays	3
The Three Colonels	6
The Reverend Blomefield	7
The Oxford and Cambridge Incident	9
Haynes' Garage	10
Skills	13
Chapel	18
Entertainment	20
Church	22
Working the Land	26
Horse Keeping	27
Allotments	28
The Brook	32
Bells	34
Pubs	35
Sherington Feast	40
Article by Jack Ivester Lloyd	45
Wartime	47
Prisoner of War Camp	49
The Home Guard	51
Organists	53
Footpaths	54
Teddy Griffin	56
Ben Line	57
Jack Pateman	58
Kit Clare	60
Trees on the Knoll	61
Thatching	62
Artists	63
Timber Merchants	70
Horses	74
Building of the Motorway	77

SCAN 78

Toffees 80

SHEFCO 81

Transport 83

Thumbsticks 85

The Blue Bridge 88

Manor Farm 90

The Mound 91

Hymn Book Comments 93

C. H. Smith & Sons Ltd 97

Trees 98

Pipelines 100

Final Snippets 101

Foreword

Norman Arnold started the Sherington Historical Society in the year 2000 to ensure that the history of the village was not lost. He recruited a small band of like-minded people to set about documenting the history of the village and researching events prior to those in living memory. Our local group is growing slowly and steadily, and now consists of about 40 members.

Philip Smith, the author of this book, was born in 1927 and is often called the unofficial Mayor of Sherington, due to the fact that he has lived in and cared for the village all his life. He has often commented that the only time he left Sherington was when he joined the army to fight for his country during the Second World War.

This book is Philip's second publication, the first being *Sherington Voices*, which contained transcriptions of interviews recorded by Philip with some residents of Sherington, and has long been out of print.

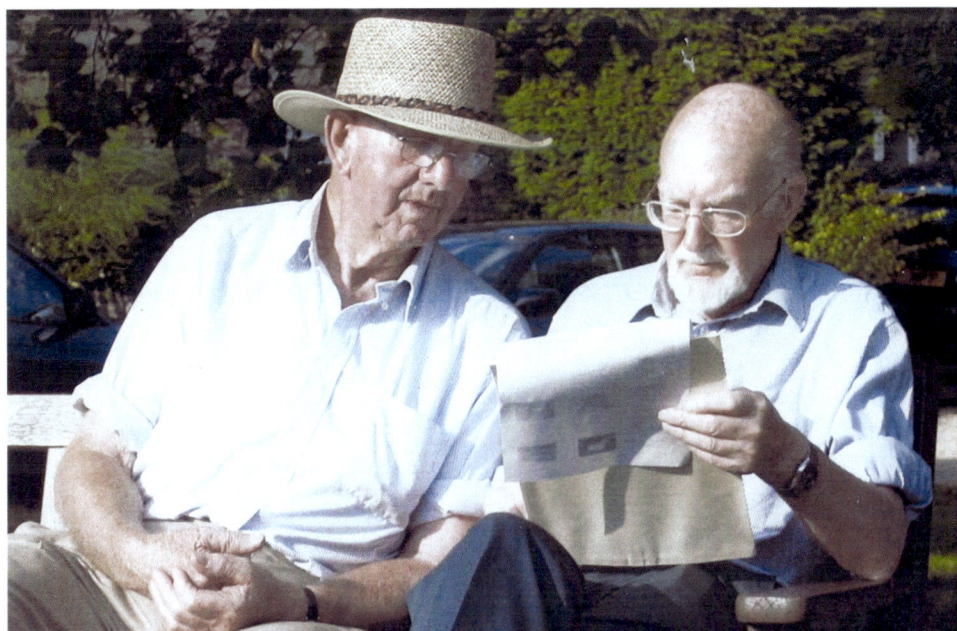

The author (left) with Norman Arnold, founder of Sherington Historical Society (photo taken in 2005)

This book, *A Little Bird Told Me...*, is a wonderful look back on village life through Philip's eyes and to the people he loved and respected. He is at pains to stress that this is not his story, but the story of others. I think through his words we can all see the love Philip has for this small North Buckinghamshire village.

I was one of those people that Norman Arnold recruited in the original group of villagers who started the Sherington Historical Society. Norman died in 2006. I'm sure he would have been actively involved in the making of this book if he had still been with us, and that he would have been very proud to have been associated with it.

Mark Vale
Chairman
Sherington Historical Society
January 2013

Preface

The stories as written in this publication belong to those characters that lived amongst us hereabouts, and retailed such as they went about their daily routine, and who sought no profit or gain from their dialogue.

Like all yarns and incidents there is bound to be a stretch of the imagination, but in the telling of them, they brought amusement, laughter and some disbelief. But one could say that Harry Smith summed it up adequately by declaring, "I shall always tell you the truth 'til it suits me better to tell a lie."

After a lifetime here amongst them, it has been a privilege and a pleasure to record these memories, and the writer holds himself totally, and without reserve, responsible for any offence or distress caused for any reason.

My thanks, unbounded and unlimited to the following friends, because these words would never have reached the general public were it not for Betty Feasey M.B.E., who at all times met my demands in the transcribing of my clumsy notes.

And David and Liz Revell who gathered the whole lot together and made it what it is now.

And certainly not least, my old friend Gerald Stratton of Newport Pagnell, professional journalist and editor, who encouraged the production by saying, "Don't talk about it, get on and write it."

We love the place, O God
Wherein thine honour dwells
The joy of thine abode
All earthly joy excels.

Hymn Nº 242. A & M.

God moves in a mysterious way
His wonders to perform
He plants his footsteps in the sea
And rides upon the storm

Hymn Nº 181.
A & M revised

Dedicated to the memory of
Juanita Mary Smith

In the Beginning

Life's a journey, but it doesn't hurt to stop and have a look at things on the way. So said the village sage, of which there were many over the years. It doesn't seem to matter where in the world the journey takes place 'cos some walks are just as important as others, or maybe less, whichever.

The centre of this story is in the North Buckinghamshire village of Sherington, in the deanery of Newport Pagnell and the diocese of Oxford. It has a church, a school, a public house and a village hall, supported by a population of approximately one thousand subjects – just far enough away from a massive conurbation that allows it to maintain its independence and the individual characters that go with it. Needless to say, those characters are fast dying out, and before they disappear altogether it may be just as well to record the habits and stories of some of them – all a star in their own way.

This particular journey starts on New Year's Day, nineteen hundred and twenty-seven, when Harry and Ann Smith were gifted of a son to go with their current family of two elder girls and a boy.

Newport Road, Sherington in the 1900s

Calves End circa. 1920s

Their home at that time was Osbourne Villa in Calves End, now known as Crofts End. What Harry was doing living in a villa, one pondered, he being a horse vehicle carrier in his formative years of one-man business, graduating to a First War ex-army ambulance of Crossley manufacture in the late twenties. His next door neighbour but one was the local policeman P. C. Knibbs, locally known as 'Knibbo', and Knibbo was no fool and knew thereabouts what was going on in the village. He had served in the south of the county and came here from Lillingstone Dayrell. It was about that time when Harry suffered severely from a bout of rheumatic fever and was very ill. Thus Knibbo paid him a visit on his way to make his first point on duty in the next 30 minutes. Harry's wife shooed him upstairs to the patient's bedside. "How are you Harry?" said the police constable. "Dreadful, I'm gonna die – oh, hold my head up please, Knibbo." So Knibbo put his arm under Harry's head and he fell back on the pillow and went fast asleep, trapping the

P.C. Knibbs pictured with other members of the Bucks Constabulary in the 1920s

P.C. Knibbs with his bicycle at the junction
of the High Street and Calves End

policeman's arm. The slightest effort to remove his arm was followed by a horrendous cry, and it was over an hour before the local copper kept his point. Harry oft-times told that story with a wink of his eye. It was during the thirties that the Swan Inn changed hands and the new landlord's name was John Thirsk Sharman Nobbs. Knibbo went in to greet the new 'mine host'. "Good evening, I'm Knibbs the policeman", to which came the reply, "Good evening, I'm Nobbs the landlord".

Schooldays

In the lifetime of present-day residents, the village has changed dramatically, in that the population then-a-day was less than five hundred compared with today's one thousand, and the village school, as we write, has twenty-five on roll, compared with one hundred plus in the thirties. There were three classes – infant, junior and senior, with one teacher to each class – headmaster, Harold Bennet Kitchen; junior class, Mrs. Winifred Furniss; infants, Miss Alice Eakins. Mr. Kitchen was resident in the schoolhouse semi-detached to the school at the rear. Mrs. Furniss cycled daily from Castlethorpe, some nine or ten miles, and was never late. Miss Eakins cycled from Wolverton and was equally

The old school house, built in 1872

Headmaster, Harold Bennet Kitchen, with pupils

punctual. Time was of the essence and the courtesy of kings. Prayers were said at morning assembly and likewise at the close of the day, with appropriate hymns according to the Biblical Calendar.

Whilst most of the children at the school lived in Sherington, quite a number lived in Chicheley, a neighbouring village, the school bus at that time being Harry's Crossley, which was an open truck during the working day, but a canopy-type 'tilt' was put on for the purpose of passenger carrying. Thus, the schoolchildren were transported under cover. One can imagine the travel during winter time. Chicheley children were obliged to bring their luncheon with them, as they were away from home from about 8 a.m. until 4.30 p.m., there being no school dinners then-a-day. Betimes, Sherington children would plunder lunch packs!

Generally speaking, the pupils would start about 4 years old and go on to 14 years, the regulation school leaving age. A few went on to either Wolverton or Newport Pagnell. Sherington children usually went home for dinner, even those who lived a mile or more distant, thus doing the journey to and fro twice a day, four miles was not uncommon.

The seasons brought a change in sport and games; snowballing to start the year, whip and top and pancake tossing, skipping to follow, and then the iron

Young Sherington ladies bathing in the River Great Ouse

5

hoops as the weather improved. Marbles followed as the sunshine and better conditions dried the road surface. By now, summer was hastening on with all its attendant outside activities, supported by the buttercups and daisies and all other flora. Onwards down the River Great Ouse, where each and every one learned to swim, and where many hours were spent enjoying the river frolics. It would be late in the evening and the shadows long, as they went up home hungry, thirsty and tired, but nevertheless happy and content with their day, with great reluctance for some, at the end of the summer, to forego their daily dip in the river. At the far end of the meadow, anchored to the bank, was the 'Ferry'. This vessel was made of heavy, timber planking and clad in corrugated sheeting with three boarded seats. Eight or nine people could sit safely in it to cross to the opposite bank by pulling a long chain through a ring. The local fishing association made and installed it, so that they could cross from one side to the other with all their gear, but the local boys also made good use of it.

The Three Colonels

Resident in Sherington at this time were the three colonels. Lt. Col. Allfrey lived with his wife at the Laurels, a large residence standing in its own grounds at the top of Calves End. Mrs. Allfrey was reported a member of Crawford's, the Irish whiskey empire. On the main road was the Lodge, where dwelt Lt. Col. Noel Byam-Grounds, a very active member of the local council. Opposite lived Lt. Col. John Clutton and his wife. Their residence was called the Small House, and was at one time the premise where Oldhams had their mineral water factory. All three gentlemen were retired from the military force. The only other distinguished notable was the Lady of Sherington Manor, Mrs. Wellesley Taylor, where again locals had it that she was related distantly to the Duke of Wellington.

The aforementioned Col. Allfrey and his wife were mainly responsible for the provision of the village hall, in that when just after the First War ended, some form of a memorial was suggested, the Colonel offered the thought of a memorial hall, and if that proposal carried, he would cover half the cost if the village raised the balance. It followed that the hall was built with the sum of £800, and the Allfrey family honoured their commitment. The hall was completed in 1927 and has been the nerve centre for all those years.

The Reverend Blomefield

At the time this story started, i.e. the late nineteen twenties, the rector here was the Reverend Henry Arthur Gilbert Blomefield M.A., and he and his family lived in what is now the old rectory. His living was Sherington St. Laud's church, and he was to be the minister here for over 30 years. Every Sunday saw at least two services: morning service at 11 a.m. and evensong at 6 p.m. There was a good choir, accompanied by a very efficient pipe organ. A team of ringers were in attendance to call the worshippers to their holy orders, two churchwardens always on duty and, of course, the sexton. What heavy responsibility he held – unlock the church, then the rector's vestry, stoke the furnace in the 'stokehole', and in addition to that, stoke the large tortoise stove, a coke-burner that stood in the nave towards the north door. Those who sat closest were the warmest, but also had to contend with the heavy fumes betimes.

Reverend Henry Arthur Gilbert Blomefield

*Oxford and Cambridge undergraduates taking an
'oath of friendship', February 1935*

*The procession of undergraduates through Sherington after their
'peace conference', February 1935*

As aforesaid, the population was less than 500 in Sherington, and it follows that over the Reverend's long incumbency, he knew personally nearly all the residents, welcoming the newborns at their baptism and later in their lives saw them in his church at their wedding ceremony, only to repeat the performance with their newborns. How well the outbreak of the 39/45 War is remembered, because on that fateful day we choirboys went in church for the 11 a.m. divine service, and as we came out at noon we were met by some of the older ladies of the village, who informed us that war had been declared by the Prime Minister, Mr. Neville Chamberlain, over the radio. This was devastating news to those mothers who had seen the ravages of the Great War just over 20 years earlier, an experience from which the country had hardly recovered. The natural maternal emotions were manifest, and many a tearful lady went homeward.

The Oxford and Cambridge Incident

It was during the Reverend Blomefield's time that we saw the Oxford and Cambridge incident. 'Twas on 24th February 1935, when a large delegation from each of those university cities entered the village to meet together on the Knoll, the name by which our village green is known. Both parties had some very serious business to conduct. It seems that some time before, certain assertions and accusations had been made, and it festered an ill feeling of such magnitude that a high level order came to dark and light blues, that they should meet on neutral ground to settle their differences in a courteous and peaceful manner. Vast crowds were on hand, many travelling long distances to witness the truce. And so it was that the chosen couple of students, one from Cambridge holding a copy of 'The Cam', their college rag, the other from Oxford holding his copy of 'The Isis', met in Sherington. Holding both copies under the village pump, they let the water flow and wash away all and any ill feeling, that peace should follow from that day forward. They released a dove of peace that fluttered its wings over the gathering and made off in the distance. That it was a dove was contested by one old villager, whose loud voice could be heard declaring, "Why, it's a bloody pigeon". The village made national news the next day with photos of the ceremony on the Knoll on most front pages. The reason Sherington was chosen as the meeting place was because we are exactly halfway between the two cities, it being 45 miles to each from here.

Haynes' Garage

At the time of the ceremony on the Knoll just mentioned, Mr. C. J. Haynes' garage was in its early stages. His premises consisted of a row of thatched cottages standing where the present garage stands, and when he started his engineering business some of the cottages were occupied – the Warren family and 'Topper' Brown being well remembered to date. He had two petrol pumps, hand operated of course, and petrol in those days was about 1/9d per gallon (today's prices: approximately 9 new pence a gallon or 2 new pence a litre). Motor cars were rare in the village in those days, but Messrs. Haynes catered for them all, whatever the demands. A highly-skilled mechanical engineer, Mr. Haynes could turn his hand to any problem, even to making his own 'cat's whisker' wireless

Mr. C. J. Haynes, the founder of Haynes' Garage & Transport, at the footplate. His son, Tom, is the small boy.

Haynes' first fleet of lorries

set, a rare bird in those days. He originated from Leighton Buzzard, where he was employed as a steamroller driver by a contractor of that town, who hired such equipment out to local councils, namely L. B. Faulkner, who was also into boat building on the Grand Union Canal, which was a very busy transport waterway at that time. It followed that the North Bucks surveyor hired a roadroller from Faulkner, and Mr. Haynes was the driver, and that's what brought him here. Carrying out running repairs in his spare time, he soon realised that he had to go full time, and so he made the plunge.

Ably supported by his wife in his new enterprise, he prospered, finally acquiring the row of cottages and the thatched house on the corner of the main road. Such was his business acumen, that he started a transport company, and by the end of the thirties his haulage fleet was a very important facility in the district. Just before the outbreak of the Second War, he demolished the cottages and built the garage that we see today, his two daughters and two sons all being employed within the two companies. After the War, Messrs. Haynes and Co. bought the old cottage standing nearby and built the transport garage alongside. Both service garage and transport garage are currently managed by the third and fourth generation of Haynes. Story has it that when the Haynes' fleet of lorries got too large for the existing yard, they would park up in

Haynes' lorries and garage today

the White Hart yard overnight. Oft-times they were loaded overnight with hot tarmacadam, and the warmth would attract the poultry, and they would roost on the rear axle of the vehicle, under cover and nicely warm. Next morning, Blackburn Jack was in High Wycombe with his load of tarmac, tipped it up only to discover five pullets perched on the back axle. The rest of the story is left to the reader's imagination. One can only admire the enterprise and the daring of such men who were successful by their own efforts and skills.

As a conclusion to those early years, when Mr. Haynes finally demolished the cottage row, that saw the end of the village reading room, a facility provided by one of the smaller dwellings for use of residents who could go and read a library book, or a magazine, and so on, a much-valued recreation before the village hall came about.

There were a few more motors and vans getting about by this time; Charlie the nurseryman being one of them. He ambitiously drove his van up to Covent Garden, London for his flowers. His van had three forward gears, but time came to replace it, and the later model he bought had four forward gears, but nobody told Charlie, and for many miles he went about his travels using only three of his four forward gears until all was revealed. The same man who couldn't get his motor to start one evening got someone to give him a tow, and when he got it going, he left it running all night so he knew he could get on in the morning without delay.

Another village character visited relations in far-away Nottinghamshire, and whilst there they gave him a piano, so, not to miss the chance of a bargain, he loaded it on the car running board, tying it to the door handle, and brought it home to Sherington, giving a tune in Market Harborough on the way.

Skills

The skills possessed within small communities can be impressive and no less in Sherington. In a document published in the year 1798, the following information was given – referred to as Sherington men – gentlemen, farmers, cordwainers, matmakers, blacksmith, tailors, lacemakers, plasterers, poulterers, victuallers, carpenters, mason, carriers, wheelwrights, gardeners, bakers, parish clerks, servants and labourers. Most of those talents were manifest in the course of the generations right through the 1800s, 1900s, and even to the present day.

Local builders, possibly Sherington men

If we take the matmakers for example, then one is referring very much to a local industry. The main material was the river rushes, gained from the Great Ouse within Sherington waters. Men and women would wade in to waist depth, cutting the rushes just below the water line and bundle them, tying them with a rush rope. The rushes were then brought up the village on a cart and laid out to dry, usually on the

Bundles of rushes attached to a wall beam for plaiting – the plaiter walks backward away from the beam as the work grows in length (drawing by Charles Stephens)

Rush backing to the seat in the White Hart

grass of the Knoll, and then taken into store. Not only mats were made, but chair seats were very much part of the production line. It is on record that a Mr. Bunker, who lived up Church End and what is now Park Road, would have a stack of several dozen chair frames out in the road waiting for him to apply the rush seating. The said chair frames were made in High Wycombe and came up to this village by railway. Other products were the bags that the labourers used to carry their food and drinks. Shoulder straps allowed them to be worn as they walked at plough and the like, or they would hang them on the horses' hames [a part of the harness]. A rush bag apparently could 'breathe' and kept its contents amazingly fresh. Rush backing was also applied as an insulation to wooden seating and was fixed to the wall; when the drinkers leaned back to the wall, one could feel the warmth. A good example of that can be seen in the room on the right in the White Hart public house.

As late as the 1930s, the reed cutters would come with their lorry from St. Neots and spend days in the summer reed cutting and take them back to St. Neots where, we were told, the rushes were placed between the curved boards that made the beer barrels as a sealant. We couldn't understand why, with the River Great Ouse running through their native town, they came to the same river some twenty-five miles away. Probably our rushes were more suitable?

Of carpenters, one such was Joe Pikesley, one-time village undertaker. His premises were the red-brick extension on the roadside end of the property now called 'Harriets End'. It is said that when a body was taken for burial, they would carry it up the footpath across the two fields to the church, thus saving the shilling fee that was charged for the use of the village bier – the hand truck conveyance used for that purpose.

When mentioning the wheelwrights of the village, one immediately thinks of Mr. George Hine, whose reputation was highly regarded throughout the Midland area. His work as a cart maker could be seen all over the county, and he was a prize winner at many an agricultural show. We have written evidence of him and Mr. Middleweek showing a new cart at Bedfordshire County Show at Ampthill, taking first prize,

*G. J. Hine's wheelwrights — photo taken from the Knoll
looking up Church Road*

A Hine's cart

and selling both horse and cart on the showground to finish the day. Mr. Hine and his family were devout chapel members, and he was the senior elder of the Wesleyan chapel on the Knoll, just across the road from his home and workshop. Some say he took his service to Our Lord to great extremes and wouldn't take a Sunday paper under any condition, but his belief in his maker was unbounded.

Several times a week and oft-times a day, Mr. Hine would be seen somewhere about the chapel. In those days, there were many duties, such as the water to be turned off and the fire stove to be cleaned ready for Sunday, the hymn board listed, and so many of the incidentals to which he paid attention, and, of course, the preacher for the next service was to be appointed for both morning and evening services. If the visitor had travelled a long journey, then it was expected that they would be entertained for lunch and tea, and so it is true to say that Mr. George Hine was in charge of all such things. One story still lingers about when the Oakley hunt met on the Knoll. Away they went and put in up Gun Lane, where they soon found their fox and chased him

The Oakley hunt meeting on the Knoll with Hine's wheelrights in the background on the right

down towards the village, and in order to find refuge, the fox made for the wheelwright's shop, and through the open door of the workshop went 'Reynard'. About five minutes before, one of the workmen had varnished a newly-finished cart, and it follows that the varnish was still wet. In went the fox, closely followed by the hounds in full cry. The fox jumped up on to the overhead shelving with hounds leaping up for their prey. Dust and shavings filled the air, as did the comments of the workforce – one can imagine the state of the newly-varnished cart. The fox jumped clear of hounds only to live another day, and ever after, if hounds met at Sherington, Mr. Hine ordered the doors to be kept closed!

Chapel

The Wesleyan chapel was well attended at that time and held together a very friendly loyal band within the village. Meanwhile, the Congregational chapel round in Calves End was also a very important place of worship. Built in 1822, it had within its complex a small cottage either side. It is said that the cottages were an afterthought because the roof on the main building was so heavy it put a strain on the outside

Congregational chapel

Congregational chapel Sunday school, 1911

Charlie Nursaw with his family

walls and was likely to push them out, so the cottages were added to help strengthen the walls against that likelihood. The chapel caretaker lived within at a reduced rent, one tenant to clean the inside each week and the other to gather firing, clean the tortoise stove, keep the building suitably heated and attend Sunday worship as well. The head man of that chapel was Mr. Charlie Nursaw, who had, with his wife, eight daughters and one son. It was Mr. Nursaw who saw that the chapel was licensed for marriages, as clearly he had a very close interest in such things with his large family of girls! How he coped, cycling to work each day; in the evening doing his garden, mending the family shoes, he also has a very large allotment garden and still attended worship twice on Sunday. All his family did very well in the outside world other than the only boy, Bert, who joined the army before the Second War and died as a result of active service during the war years.

Entertainment

"One singer, one song", the cry would go up in any of the three pubs of a Saturday night. The lady at the piano was a housewife with a large family, and her time was taken up in looking after their demands, but just on Saturday night she would accompany her husband and go to the local. She was most unusual at the piano, playing mainly on black notes and always by ear and was never ever seen with a musical score. It didn't matter what they wanted, once they hummed it over she would accompany them. Most vocalists had their special song, and woe betide the rogue who dared to take it over. Darky always sang 'Sweet Adeline' and Sedgy gave them 'Spring Time in the Rockies'. Jack would offer 'The Isle of Capri', but always with a much emphasised 'HH' before the isle, so what you heard was 'The Hisle of Capri'. Harry protected his piece with every care. His was 'The Farmers Boy', and he got quite het up were someone to help him out other than during the chorus! Ole Lil offered 'Love's Old Sweet Song'. It was sung in a pleasant enough voice, but she did have trouble with her false teeth and always on that top note. On the crucial 'And I'll be there', down would drop her top set, but she always was awarded a good round of applause. Occasionally

Carol singers in Sherington

Dusty would render 'The Pride of Old Flanagan's Band', and when it came to the part where the drums bang, bang, the cornets rang and the trumpets blaze away, he demonstrated them all – marching up and down in step to the beat. The pleasure this 'off-the-cuff' performance gave was abundant, and whilst the performers may not have got further bookings they were certainly appreciated on the night. There was just one outstanding singer amongst the community, and such was his prowess at classical singing he won the gold medal at the National Eisteddfod in Wales, held that year in Aberystwyth. He came to the village when he married the local hairdresser. He was born in the Rhondda Valley of Wales in a town called Tonypandy. Long Un's son, Bill, didn't take any gold medal for his contribution, but when called upon for his turn, all the ladies paid attention 'cos his party piece was entitled 'That's What God Made Mothers For'. Oh, how he played on the sentiment of that last passage, which goes as follows: 'She'll do all she can to make you a man and she'll wave you goodbye at the door, She'll sigh for you, Cry for you, Yes, even die for you, That's what God made Mothers for.' Loud was the applause for Bill ..."Have another, Bill ... Drink up!"

Church

The village church is named St. Laud's, after a French bishop of no apparent consequence, who it seemed attended a parochial church council meeting here and there, and that's about all. St. Laud's stands on an eminence and has a square tower in height 62 feet. The tower holds five bells that are hung in the original oak frame with the ringing chamber halfway up the sixty or more stone steps that lead to the manhole cover atop of the tower. The clock is driven by stone weights that must be wound up daily, one weight for the timepiece and one for the hourly chime. The entrance to the tower is gained by the door that stands on the steps under the clock.

An interesting feature is the sundial engraved in the buttress to the right of the organ door. Entering the porch and passing through the 14th century pair of doors, one is welcomed by a well-lit building, much of the light is shed through the large clear west window. Standing under

St. Laud's church

Sundial on the buttress by the organ door of the church

Interior of St. Laud's church looking towards the altar

the west window and looking to the east, one sees a fine stained glass depiction of the Adoration and another of John the Baptist. From west to east, the three split levels give a pleasant elevation to the altar. In the chancel, one may observe the Brevington pipe organ, completely restored during 2009/2010 by Messrs. Peter Collins, the well-known organ builders from Melton Mowbray. 'Tis a single manual with a very pleasing sound, and is perfectly adequate for the demands of the worshippers.

During the 1900s, for many years the sexton was from the well-known and long-established Watts family. Tom Watts was legendary in so many ways. He, being tall in stature, was locally known as 'Long Un'. He portrayed all that one would imagine of a village character, capable of so many village crafts. Not for Long Un was the high education standards, but he could thatch a rick or house, lay a hedge, mow the grass with his scythe, and, of course, being sexton he was also the grave digger. He could be found in the White Hart any time during opening hours, and sometimes during closing hours as well. He never missed Sunday dinner time, he went straight in from morning service, and he would have a full session until two o'clock. Those who attended six o'clock evensong were met with a strong pungent smell of beer as Long Un handed out the hymn books, and one lady of 'cut glass stamp' used to regularly cough her heart up as she stood within breathing distance of the sexton. When the stone wall fell down that surrounded the graveyard, the rector of the day questioned Long Un as to why he hadn't rebuilt it. He replied,

Tom Watts, known as Long Un

"Well, it's like this here, them as are in can't get out, and them as are out don't worn't to goo in." Whenever he was asked if he wanted another drink, he would never refuse. "You mustn't goo agin the house", he would say, alluding that the pub was there to sell beer and to refuse was not good for trade. "Ah, when I'm gone, come and give me a stamp and I shall hear yer." He meant stamp above the grave and he would hear down below. His fellow ringers would swear he rang the third bell as he slept at the rope. Every villager had his favourite song, and Long Un always sang 'Sailor Boy'. Ah, ole pipe-smoking Long Un will linger long in the memory of this village.

Many of Long Un's family have married in St. Laud's, and the photograph on the previous page shows Long Un on the occasion of the wedding of his granddaughter, Barbara Watts, to Roland Smith in 1952.

Roland Smith and Barbara Watts, newly
married, outside St. Laud's church,
23rd August 1952

Working the Land

The feudal system in this country still held good, even during the 1920s and 30s. Country folk didn't change their jobs all that often; many of the cottages were occupied with a condition that they were tied to the workers' occupancy as long as the employment lasted. No job, no home, as was the case with the farm worker and his tied cottage, many of whom spent the whole of their working life on the one farm. These men of the rural scene had enjoyed the benefit of the Education Act of 1872 and could ably read and write within certain limits. They were not into map reading and the like, so with the morning orders reference was made to the fields by name. In our parish of 1,850 acres, the fields had the most delightful of names. Starting from Cross Albans would be Great Dene, Little Dene, Long Dole, the Slype, Wynyards, Dry Banks, Perry Barn, Little Perry, Bedlam Spinney, Little Stocking, New Pasture, Far Side, Basin's Piece, the Planks, Ray Meadow, Grooms Hole, Burnt Hills, Townsend, Cow Pasture, Lordsmead, Bottom Meadow, Cut-throat Spinney, Bakers, Mare Hill, Cold Harbour, Price's, and so on.

George Fleet (in the saddle), Arthur Borton (left) and Tom Watts (right)

The workforce on the farm would be made up of the horse keeper, the stockman, the ploughman, and the feathered friends would have a poultry maid who dealt with the watering and feeding of the hens and the egg collection. The workmen would possess the skills necessary to build a rick, milk the cows, lay a hedge, thatch the rick, clean the ditches, mend the fences etc. They took their food with them in the rush shoulder bag, and their canteen was very often under the thickest and warmest bush in the hedgerow. Those men who worked with horses had a caring love for their charge and would treat those hardworking animals with every consideration. Oft-times, the men would have no-one to talk to, so the horse would be spoken to as if it was a human being. Early mornings were the order of the day, a 6 a.m. start with most horse keepers, and that for six of the seven days of the week, but they went in to feed on Sunday morning somewhat later, say about 7 a.m. It is said that the ploughman would walk ten miles in a day should he cover an acre of land, the horses doing likewise but with the additional burden of pulling the plough.

Horse Keeping

One of the rewards of horse keeping and stables was the resultant manure, always welcome to the gardener and horticulturist, it was mostly a give-away commodity, rarely a small charge was made. Great pride was taken in the size and quality of the fruits and roots and berries at harvest time. The allotment holders were probably the most enthusiastic, their bounty being a very important part of the housekeeping budget. The parents with a large family were rarely, if ever, to buy vegetables or fruit from the local shop, they being quite skilled in the preserving of all culinary requirements, including eggs which were preserved in a bucket of 'water glass'. It was their proud boast that they would have enough to last them till apples came again, the time-piece in the gardening calendar to be 'when

Jack and Amy Pateman 'up the 'llotment'

you hear the cuckoo'. A very important bird song was the first cuckoo call, and always most welcome in that it brought better weather and, of course, fresh green stuff to the table. As the Good Book tells us, 'Seed time and Harvest shall not fail'.

One of the sources of horse manure at that time was from Village Farm, where lived Ern the horse dealer, and by definition he always had a muck heap in the yard. Time was he had a surplus, so he mentioned to Harry that he had a load of manure in the way and could he do with it? Harry readily accepted and told Jack about it, and Jack agreed to buy it for half-a-crown, he to collect it. Later that day, Fred said to Harry, "I hear you have a load of muck for sale." "Yes," came the reply, "It will cost you half-a-crown." So Harry sold the one load of muck to two different men. The following Saturday, Jack borrowed a farm cart to collect the muck and Fred had done exactly the same, so they both turned up at Ern's together for the same load of muck. After some consultation, they both went to Harry's house and confronted him about the situation and on the issue that he had sold a load of muck twice to two different men. "Well," said Harry, "I shall only sell that load to you two, and if anybody else wants to buy it I shall refuse them." And at that he bid them good afternoon and closed the door, leaving the two men in utter bewilderment to sort the matter out between them.

Allotments

The custody of the allotments at that time rested with the village rector, and he drew up his own rules and regulations to be most strictly adhered to by all, a copy of which reads as follows:

RULES AND REGULATIONS

RESPECTING THE RENT AND MANAGEMENT OF THE

ALLOTMENTS OF LAND

LET TO THE INHABITANTS OF SHERINGTON, BUCKS,

BY THE REV. J. C. WILLIAMS, RECTOR

1. The Land is to be let for the term of one Year only; when, without notice, it falls into the hands of the Landlord, and possession will be given on the 11th of October in each year to approved Tenants.

2. The Rent is to be paid in Five equal monthly payments; the first payment to be made on the first Monday in April, and the remaining payments respectively on the first Monday in each succeeding month of May, June, July, and August.

3. The Land is to be cultivated in the following manner:- namely, one third, and no more, with potatoes; one third and no more, with wheat, barley, or any other kind of grain; and the remaining third, with cabbages, peas, beans, carrots, or any other green crop.

4. Each person's allotment is to be divided into three equal parts on entry; and every person must cultivate, with the same course of cropping, a similar division of his Land, to that used for the three respective modes of cultivation above mentioned, by the other Tenants.

5. Any occupier neglecting the cultivation of his Land will not be allowed to re-take it at the end of the current year in which the neglect may take place.

6. No person shall be allowed to sub-let his Land, or in any way to transfer it to another Tenant.

7. The Land is to be cultivated by spade-husbandry only.

8. No occupier, who is at work for any employer, will be allowed to work upon his Land after six o'clock in the Morning, or before six o'clock in the Evening, without special permission from his employer.

9. Each person is to keep his own allotment of fence in good repair, and the ditches properly open.

10. Any occupier convicted before a Magistrate of poaching, or of any other act of dishonesty; or proved, by evidence to the satisfaction of the Rector, to have committed any act of dishonesty, shall be dispossessed of the occupation of his Land, and his crop be taken at a valuation.

11. Every occupier shall attend public worship at the Parish Church, at least once every Sunday; and should he neglect so to do, without sufficient cause, he shall be dispossessed of his Land.

12. If any occupier shall become a drunkard, or a frequenter of public houses, or in any respect a disorderly person, he shall be dispossessed of his land.

13. No person is to trespass upon another's Land in going to and from his own allotment.

14. No occupier is to work on his Land on the Lord's Day, or remove the produce after eight o'clock in the morning of that Day.

15. The Land must be manured each year with the whole of the manure arising from the cropping, and with as much more as it may be convenient to the Tenant to provide.

16. Baths and such drains as are beneficial to the occupiers generally, shall be made and repaired at the joint expense of the occupiers.

17. If any dispute arise respecting the meaning of the above Rules, or any other subjects connected with the occupation of the Land, the affair is to be referred to the Rector, whose decision shall be absolute and final.

** It is necessary to add that these Rules will be rigidly enforced, and special attention is directed to the 10th, 11th, and 12th.

SHERINGTON RECTORY; October, 1847

[CURTIS, TYP. NEWPORT PAGNELL]

Peter 'Birdie' Mynard: Olney born, he came to Sherington to find his wife, Mary, upon demob from the army – he has been an allotment holder for 61 years

Sherington allotments today – originally they stretched as far as the trees on the horizon

At the time of writing there are but few allotment holders, they numbering single figures, where between the wars there were many dozens. Of Ern, the horse dealer, it was said he was a regular attendee at the famous Barnet Horse Fair in North London, and on one occasion was offered seven donkeys that a dealer had brought over from Ireland, but couldn't find a buyer. Ern said he didn't really want them, but he would give five shillings each for them and that's all. The Irishman rejected such a silly offer out of hand, but it seems a few days later the Irishman walked into Village Farm yard with seven donkeys on a long reign and said to Ern, "Here you are, I couldn't find a better offer, so I've walked all the way from Barnet, and you can have 'em at your price."

The Brook

Most villages had a brook or ditch or water course into which ran the surface water, thus giving a running supply of soft water which, it seems, the housewife preferred when doing the week's washing, so often in the wash house wherein was the copper, usually a five-gallon vessel under which was a fire grate for the purpose of heating the water. The brook had other purposes, of course. It was known that in Water Lane some of the women had their own dipping hole, where the hole was just large enough to take an ordinary bucket or pail. Most valuable was that bucket of water, because it saved going to the pump or the well, it being fit for all purposes other than human consumption, although there are some

The brook in Water Lane

reservations about that. The brook also grew fresh watercress, where many a bunch would appear on the table during the summer. "Ah, you gotta hev some cress 'cos of the iron," old Lizzie would say, who in her eighties had never been to the dentist, had a full set of teeth, which she cleaned with soot from the chimney once a week. A lovely smile had Lizzie. Most menfolk took water from the brook for the garden and the like, and all cattle and sheep etc. would refresh themselves from it; equally, the horse keeper would take his charge for to quench its thirst. The brook in general terms had its usefulness and was regarded as a good friend, but there came times when it wasn't so. In the spate of a cloudburst, the water would rise over its bank and often caused household flooding, some houses having several inches of flood water within its walls, the smell of which lingered long after the water had receded. Many a boat race was held on the brook. Coming home from school, the boys would gather small lengths of straw just a few inches long, and they were the 'boats'. With great eagerness, the boats would enter the underground pipes or tunnels, then there was a rush to the other end to see which one emerged first.

The mothers used to warn their young family not, under any circumstances, to ever drink the water from the brook. "And if you do, you'll die." Alec Wright was a well-remembered old character who lodged with old Gran Warren and worked at Fences Farm, Tyringham. He walked down early in the morning and back about 6 p.m. in the evening. One hot summer's day, he came up as the boys were playing in the brook with an old biscuit tin. Alec looked down to the boys and said, "Give us a guzzle of that water in the tin", so one of the number gave Alec the tin of water, which he gulped down, his old Adam's apple going up and down like a plunger. When he had drunk of it, he handed the tin back with a glow of satisfaction and went on his way, much to the disappointment of the boys who expected him to drop down dead, having disregarded their mother's warning that anyone drinking the brook water would die on the spot.

Alec Wright was one of many workmen who walked to work, oft-times quite a distance. One man who lived in the chapel cottages walked to Tickford Park to work every day, always the shortest route across the fields, but still some five or six miles, and Piddington Bill, who courted a lady from Piddington, near Northampton, would only see her once a week, and he always walked to Piddington for his weekly courtship, some ten miles each way. They eventually married, so she came to live here, thus saving Bill his weekly journey.

Bells

One of the unusual features of everyday life in the village was the one o'clock bell. The bell was rung from the ringing chamber in St. Laud's church, bell number one, known as the treble, it being the highest tone. It was rung from 12.55 for five minutes and was heard as far as the parish boundary, about a mile radius from the church. The workforce in the fields would hear its ring and therefore know that it was time for the midday break. The duty rested with the sexton or his deputy, and in Long Un's case it was normally his daughter, Mary, who rung it. It was surprising, on a clear day, just how far its call could be heard. The practice ceased at the outbreak of the 39/45 War and was never resumed. Another weekly bell-ringing habit was a different kind; it was a hand bell and was rung by Mick Mazzone, very well-known tradesman in the district. He and his family ran the fish and chip shop in the town centre of Newport Pagnell, and during the day he went round the villages with a pony and dray selling fruit and veg, and sometimes wet fish. Stopping at various points in the parish, he would ring the hand bell for a minute of two, and very soon the housewives would be at the dray gathering their needs for a reasonable price. Mick would be outside the school at playtime, and was known to sell the boys half of a pomegranate for a halfpenny and give them the necessary pin to go with it. It seems wherever there was a penny to be made, then Mick was on to it. In the heavy floods along the Newport road, travelling on a bike was an impossibility, and Mick would be there with his flat-bottomed trolley, horse driven, and the cyclist would get up with their bikes and they

St. Laud's church

would be taken through the deep-flooded section for a penny or two, whatever. Of Italian origin and parentage, Mick Mazzone was a most valuable part of Newport's community. Boys from the villages knew his value too, for on a Friday night they could catch Bob Wesley's bus into town for a penny, have a penn'orth of chips from Mick's chip shop, into the pictures for threepence, a penn'orth of bullseyes from Charlie Mynard's sweet shop – all the lot inside a sixpence.

Pubs

Before 1923 there were four pubs in the village. Namely, the Royal Oak in Church End, the White Hart in Gun Lane, the Swan Inn on the main road and the Crown and Castle, also on the main road. The Royal Oak closed in the 20s, but the others have survived, albeit a somewhat chequered history. The Crown and Castle kept open until 1961/2. In recent years, we saw the closure of the White Hart for nearly two years, and it was re-opened following a public enquiry that was held in the borough council offices in Milton Keynes. The Swan Inn closed for refurbishment, re-opened and then closed again. And so, in the lifetime of this generation, the village has gone from four to one pub. The brewery serving the White Hart was Hopcraft and Norris, a Brackley company and one wonders, in those days before motor transport, how in all weathers the drayman with his pair of horses and wagon endured the weary journey from that Northamptonshire town to this village, some twenty-five miles each way. Of the Swan Inn, the brewers were more local, being Charles Wells of Bedford, and that also applied to the Crown and Castle, whose brewers were Phipps of Northampton. Each pub had its own customers; a Swan man wouldn't drink in the other pubs. The beer wasn't to his taste, and the company and atmosphere was different, and the same applied to the others for the same reasons. In the better weather, for a change and a pleasant walk, some would walk 'over the hill' to the Chester Arms in Chicheley. The beer there was of a different order altogether and seemed to be more 'active'. One well-known character would say that he always undid the buttons of his braces in readiness for a sudden attack that caused him to go 'behind the hedge'. But to come back to the village there were those who had a regular

The Royal Oak — it closed in 1923

36

Mr. and Mrs. Cowley with horse and cart outside the Swan Inn, early 1900s

Meet of the Oakley hounds outside the Crown and Castle, 1905

seat, and others who were fairly good at darts, skittles or cribbage, and those who loved a sing-song on a Saturday night. And one mustn't rule out the practical joke such as the landlady who said to Bert, "Nobody ever brings me a brace of birds", following a day's shooting on the local estate. The next morning, whilst unlocking the pub, there was a brace of house sparrows hanging on the doorknob. Not a word was spoken, but there were some smiling faces about. And the other unconfirmed report of the man who was habitually late for Sunday dinner, much to the annoyance of his wife, who had to keep it hot on the saucepan top with a lid over it. One Sunday, she had had enough. He came home late as usual. "You'll find it under the lid on the saucepan", she said. He got the cloth and placed the steaming plate on the table, removed the lid to find three darts lying on the plate and nothing else. But one mustn't condemn the village pub; it was the community centre in its day, where they all met and shared each other's sorrows and joys.

The White Hart, circa. 1895, with Sarah Lawes, landlady – Mr Bailey is standing by the trap

When Harry Waterhouse kept the White Hart he would say that you could do a deal for anything from a needle to a warship in there, such was the transactions done in that place during his tenancy. Certainly the legend has it, that 'Footy' Chapman from Stoke Goldington sold a nanny goat to some American soldiers, who were stationed at Podington during the War. It was he, when visiting a patient in their sickbed, would recommend without fail a bowl of hot linseed, 'cos that is what they gave to racehorses when they were sick and ailing.

38

The White Hart in the 1960s

The White Hart today

Sherington Feast

Much of country life recognises tradition, and oft-times that goes with the patronal dedication of the local church, and St. Laud's patronal day falls around Michaelmas. In the case of this village, it was said that the original feast was the using of the summer and early autumn produce that would soon give way to the more severe weather, and so most perishable goods were used by Michaelmas (29th September) or the celebration of Harvest Festival, i.e. the Sunday nearest to 11th October. Thus, Sherington feast was usually the Saturday nearest 11th October. It was a time of much merriment. The harvest was home, the sheep had been sheared, the hay time was over and the villagers had much to be thankful for. The main narrative we have of the Victorian feasts and up to the 1914/18 War was a first-hand account from 94-year-old Joe, brother to Long Un, a man with a brilliant memory, who spoke in old Sherington dialect without any pretence. He was to tell us that the whole village rejoiced at the feast. There were stalls and roundabouts, swings and coconut shies, and one point he enlarged on was the making of spit rock. We will not go into the making of it too much, but look it up and you will learn something. The fun went on well after darkness had fallen, and Joe told us in detail how to make hand-held torches by dipping rushes from the river in a bucket of tar which, when lit with a match, would burn and give a good light for quite a long time. In the pubs, the beer was flowing with the most romantic and unbelievable stories being related. Deep into the night, the singing would be heard, as the stragglers made the frivolities last as long as they could. The following day, a Sunday, was Harvest Festival. Full to capacity would be St. Laud's with nary a spare seat, and the congregation would genuinely give thanks for a bountiful and fruitful season, and lustily would be sung the harvest hymns with emphasis on the line 'All is safely gathered in'. There was no such thing as changing the clock by an hour in those times, but the weather would soon change and sharp frosts, cold winds and snow were imminent. Thus, the Sherington feast was over for another year.

It was in later times, indeed during the 50s and 60s, that one villager got it into his head that the feast should be revived, if only just for once, and by now we were in the 1970s and Jubilee year was approaching. The person most pivotal in the setting up of the 1977 Sherington feast was Peter Gardner, a local landowner who ran Water Lane Farm and lived in the large farmhouse in Water Lane with his wife Alice and three children. In the first week in January, he called a meeting in

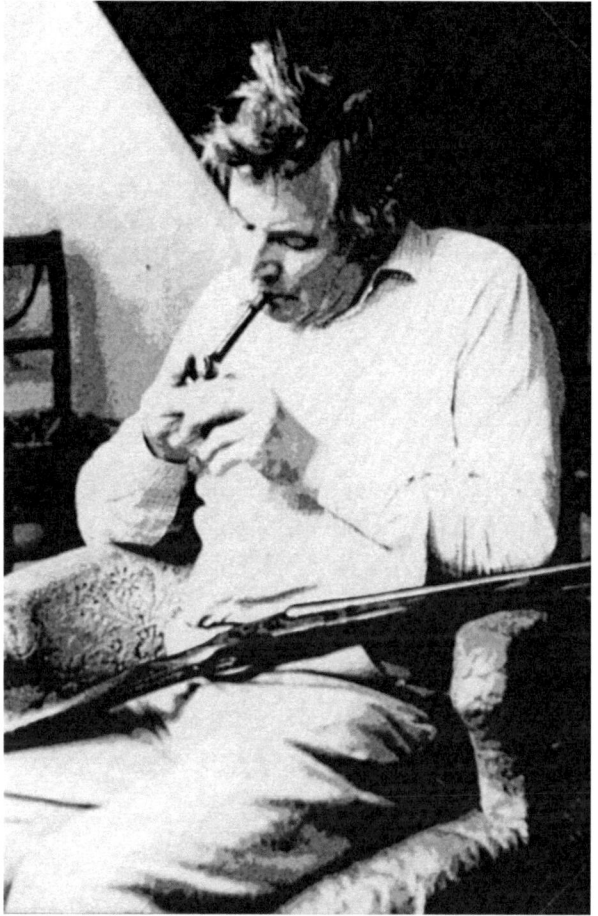

Peter Gardner

Water Lane Farmhouse, and from that meeting came a decision to run and revive Sherington feast and, to Peter's insistence, in the traditional manner. The only departure was the date. The rector of the day was the Reverend John Corfield, who threw himself into the plan with alacrity, and he found some reason why September in the long ago past was relevant, so Saturday 24th September was settled upon, and we 'opened the batting' on planning Sherington feast. What excitement, what enthusiasm and what hard work, but who cared. Meetings were held in Water Lane Farm, and two or three dozen folk were handed their responsibilities, which they all accepted without a murmur. Before long, as we ran into the summer, the feast was on the lips of all, and it seems most folk had a job somewhere on the day. Many facilities were

Peter Gardner (left) and Jack Ivester Lloyd (right) opening the Sherington feast in 1977

The author at the Sherington feast, 1977

impounded. Haynes' transport garage was central to the site, so that was readily offered, as was tractors, lorries, pick-ups, pots, pans, jerry cans; everything required on the day was offered without question.

On the Friday night of the 23rd September, the Knoll and the surrounding area was completely transformed with dozens of brightly covered stalls and tents, and whatever. It was necessary to erect a large marquee, and the village pump seemed to be an obstacle, so Peter ordered 'erect it over the pump then', and for the first time ever the village pump went under canvas. Every confidence was shown and great expectations were held, but it was a new thing as far as the organisers were concerned, albeit every member of the committee were well versed in their own right of the organising of events large and small, and many were in management of the highest level, but now the novelty of organising the success of Sherington feast laid squarely in their hands. It was important for there to be a dignitary of some repute to formally declare the feast open, and Peter was quick off the mark on that one by naming

Jack Ivester Lloyd (right) – in 1973 he wrote the article that appears on pages 45 and 46 for the Shooting Times & Country magazine

Jack Ivester Lloyd, a Sherington-born writer, countryman, author and broadcaster, at that time living in Bagley, a small town in Shropshire (see an article he wrote for the Shooting Times & Country magazine in 1973 on pages 45 and 46). Jack readily accepted the invitation, and so on that Saturday afternoon we saw the Sherington feast revived and re-enacted, very much to the organisers' dictates – no chrome, no candy floss, nothing modern, but everything traditional – the ladies in aprons and mob caps, men in boots and bowlers. The village was teeming with people from far and wide. Never were so many expected, and never were so many welcomed. What a day and what fun! Evening followed afternoon as it does, and the merriment continued with a barn dance held in Charlie Haynes' transport garage. The building took a bit of clearing up, and many a lost spanner and hammer was found in the preparations. Many songs come to mind on reflection ... 'After the Ball is Over' or 'We Could Have Danced All Night', but maybe 'The End of a Perfect Day' suits admirably. Next morning was clearing up day, and to the outstanding credit of everyone involved, by afternoon everything was restored and reinstated, and one would not have known of the events that had taken over Sherington twenty-four hours earlier. Peter and Jack Ivester Lloyd (who stayed with Peter that weekend) held the inquest on it all in the garden of Water Lane Farm: "An unforgettable experience and outstanding success, and a privilege to be invited", said Jack. "Typical Sherington", said Peter with a smug smile, as only he could, that told it all! Sherington feast revived, never to be forgotten.

Article by Jack Ivester Lloyd

Sport in my life - 2

If you were travelling from Newport Pagnell to Olney, your road would take you through the village of Sherington. Here, in that part known as Church End, my parents brought me to live. There were also, naturally, the beagles and the big tabby cat. Ma had given up her King Charles spaniels: the risk of the arrival of a Speagle or a Banniel on the scene had been too great.

By this time I was able to walk. Far enough, in fact to take a hound named Baggage on vole hunts, a sport that was a good apprenticeship to rabbiting or the bolting of foxes. The beagle bitch would find the entrance to a burrow, show it to me and then go to the bolt hole. There she waited while I poked a willow wand into the run. The voles went straight down her throat.

A wonderful brood bitch was Baggage, the mainstay of our breeding policy. She could be relied upon to produce a litter of healthy puppies every year with no trouble at all provided she was allowed to do so on our one decent easy chair. This was, of course, arranged.

There was another hound who had a hand, if that is the right word, in the breeding of what were now the Sherington Foot Beagles. Mind you, Dancer was never chosen to be a sire of puppies: he just appointed himself. Actually, he was a wonderful worker with that invaluable gift of being able to

Kennel boy

Jack Ivester Lloyd

pick up the line of a hare when she had run a hard road. But appearances were against Dancer. He was snipey about the muzzle and he had lost an eye through a particularly bad bout of distemper when a puppy for, at that time, nobody had found a preventive serum. He had a curly stern and something about his whole appearance suggested that his mother had been successfully pursued by a terrier.

However, Dancer was an enterprising chap who had an eye for the ladies, and the fact that he was small even by the standards of our pack of small hounds was no obstacle. He would conduct the bitch of his choice to a certain doorstep. I am sorry to say that in his latter years, he developed an unnatural attachment for a child's woolly lamb on wheels.

But never mind about that. The important point is that, in spite of the sires' names on several pedigrees, there was a suspicion that it should have been Dancer.

My father, having observed my vole hunting expeditions, said to me one bright Spring morning, as I was about to set off on yet another hunt with Baggage at my heels: "Ah, my boy, I see you're taking to sport." I grinned at the compliment. "Right, then! You can start to learn about beagles from the very beginning." He went into an outbuilding and emerged with a big broom. "Here, catch hold of this!"

That is how I became kennel boy to a pack of beagles and so set my foot on the first rung of a modest hunting career. The kennels at that time were a quite simple building, a lean-to affair built against the wall of Tommy Burgess's stables which formed one boundary of our yard. I learned to swill down the brick floor and change the straw on the

. . . the voles went straight down her throat . . .

45

sleeping bench and so I very soon had the duties of whipper-in added to those of kennel boy.

I quickly discovered that whipping-in was an especially arduous duty at so-called hound exercise when I was often Dad's only assistant. Most beagles have something of the imp in their make-up but this was particularly true of our pack, in its early days at least. Dad's idea of hound control was perhaps original. He just stood near the lamp post in the middle of Church End, puffing on a woodbine, quietly swearing and shouting: "Get round 'em, boy, *get round'em!"*

Doors would be slamming, women screeching about "having the law on them!" Poultry squawked, dogs barked, while I scampered into cottage gardens and even into the cottages themselves, as I tried to get our riotous hounds together again.

After we had been living at Sherington for a year or two, our beagles were put on a more orthodox footing. In this my father was greatly helped by other sportsmen of the district. The rector of the village, Parson Blomefield, whipped-in on hunting days when his duties permitted. I have since wondered how much truth there was in the story whispered to me by his younger daughter that Daddy was wearing his beagling kit under his surplice on the day he married a certain couple.

The pack was enlarged by means of what was almost a trencher-feeding system. Major Jack Taylor kept several couples of hounds at the Manor, the vicar of Emberton took a couple and

our own parson had a black-and-tan doghound named Boxer at his place.

Another very useful helper was Fred Taylor of Newport Pagnell. Fred was an outstanding sportsman and later became a Joint Master of the North Bucks Beagles as well as of the Bucks Otterhounds. However, at the time of which I am thinking, he whipped-in to the Sherington Foot Beagles and had a reputation for always being in the right spot from which to view the hunted hare. He had another useful habit; that of sending along a hundred-weight of hound-meal when it was needed.

I was a very junior whipper-in when in the hunting field. In fact, my piping rate of "Get on to 'im!" was hardly noticed, least of all by the hounds. But I could run well and, for at least one season, did so barefoot, having discovered that mud did not stick as much to flesh as to leather and there is less weight to carry. But I spent a considerable time, after getting home, in pulling thorns out of my feet.

In the early days we walked to meets and that limited the pack's range of operations. Then, one happy day, somebody – I think it was Jack Russell from Sherington Bridge – thought of Smithy's Bus. This was a ramshackle conveyance in which the owner carted anything from timber to shoppers. Smithy agreed to hire it to us on hunting days provided he drove it himself. The Master and Committee were only too willing to agree to the last-named condition; they were quite certain

the vehicle would never start or go for anyone but Smithy.

So, on a hunting morning, plenty of clean straw was put on the bottom boards of Smithy's Bus. Into this, in a safe corner, was placed a jar of beer, "just in case", as my father said. Then our section of the pack would be loaded in to be followed by my parents and myself, as well as anyone else in need of a lift. Jack Taylor and his contingent would be collected from the Manor and we set off for the meet. The two parsons came in their own cars, bringing hounds in their charge with them.

The Master and Hunt staff even sported green coats – though not the Kennel Boy. We felt that the Sherington Foot Beagles really had arrived.

2

Wartime

The outbreak of the 1939/45 War brought a dramatic change in the lives of many, no less the young men and girls of the village. When at school, they learnt of those faraway places with strange-sounding names; little did they think that one day much of their youth would be spent there. In the full bloom and flowering of their good-looking, physically active and certainly their most energetic and carefree days they were called-to-arms within weeks of the declaration. When one considers the roll of honour that is listed in some communities, we here were saddened in Herbert Charles Nursaw being our only loss of life on active service. Many of our boys served with high distinction and merit, their bravery and conduct being of the most outstanding.

We call to mind Charlie, bred and born here, joined up in 1939 with the Royal Artillery, promoted to sergeant and was mentioned in dispatches ... Ted, who schooled in Sherington and left at fourteen, joined the Royal Navy, went through officers' training and was commissioned a sub-lieutenant, thus the only Sherington schoolboy to become an officer throughout the War ... We must not leave out Bill the butcher who also went in 1939. Bill never thought that he would march many hundreds of miles through the rainforests and leeches of Burma when headmaster Charles Garret taught him of the countries of the Orient ...

Memorial plaque to Herbert Charles Nursaw in St. Laud's church

Les, who was born on the Knoll, joined the Royal Navy and was posted to the escort of the Russian Arctic convoys, and who spent many hours chopping the pack ice from the deck of the ship in order to survive the frozen wastes of the North Atlantic waters ... Douglas joined the Royal Engineers in 1943 and following the North African Campaign finished up in Italy in the Battle of Monte Cassino, he being in bomb disposal throughout his foreign service ... Ken was in the Parachute Regiment and went down from his aircraft over Caen in France, thus joining in the D-Day invasion ... Francis went as a sailor in 1944 from Water Lane and found his way round the world aboard HMS Bonaventure and later HMS Amethyst. He saw Freemantle in Australia and later sailed the Yangtse, but was demobbed before the 'Yangtse Incident'.

There were many others who gave of their best years, and brave is he that would omit the ladies who, as ever, played their part. Edna joined the ATS and reached the rank of sergeant ... as did Gwen the wheelwright's daughter ... Doreen and Kathleen went into the WRENs and Gwen, Prim's sister, joined the WAAF, as did Monica. Of course, should all ex-service personnel be listed, then a number of pages would be filled, those mentioned being just a few as an example of wartime village life and anxieties – those omitted being just as dedicated and patriotic.

In the meantime, and back here in the village, it was a matter of the old motto, 'They also serve who only stand and wait', and by that it didn't mean that the village stood still, not by any means. The Reverend Blomefield had died and a new man was appointed by the name of Reverend D. Gordon. He came with his wife and one child, a son, and they took over in the rectory. Mrs. Gordon formed a Girl Guide pack and the Reverend formed a Boy Scout troop. There was a freedom up at the rectory that we hadn't seen before; youngsters running through the house, and boys climbing trees and playing in the garden and the buildings. To aid the war effort, a waste paper campaign was started, and all the material collected was stored in one of the buildings in the top yard. It seemed before long that the popularity of the rectory exceeded that of St. Laud's, 'cos the Reverend Gordon wasn't over-popular with the laity of his church, but it could not be denied that for the young folk experiencing the pains of wartime conditions he played his part well. 'Doggy', as he was nicknamed, was fast losing his flock, and one dear lady was to tell us that for a change she would attend evensong, but on arrival noticed that she was on her own. As the hour of six o'clock approached, she began to wonder if there would be a service, but came the strike of six, the rector began the evensong and proceeded to give the service in full, four hymns included and a sermon, a one-off experience as far as we know. They said Doggy was an eccentric and of that there is little doubt. After the War, they moved away, under some pressure it is said, to South Africa, where Doggy reportedly gave good Christian service to the inhabitants of that country.

Prisoner of War Camp

At that time, there were only eight council houses in Crofts End, just the two blocks of four. Perry Lane was a cart track and was known as 'Muddy Lane', and it certainly was. Old George Borton, the council roadman, used to 'go on' regular at the Carters such as Harry, for when

Prisoner of war camp

they came down from Sherington Wood with their timber carriage, the mud would fall off the spoked wheels in quite large lumps, and it would only take three or four lumps to fill old George's barrow, so that gave him a lot of extra work. There was a footpath alongside that led up to Gowles Farm, and then on to Sherington Wood. Imagine the surprise to local villagers when it was announced that a prisoner of war camp was to be established there, and without further delay that came about. In the first place, they were German prisoners, and then followed the Italians. The encampment was heavily barbed wired, and sentry points were employed. Tight security was in force, and no fraternising allowed. The inmates were allowed out to work on local farms under supervision and armed guard. As time passed, the hard discipline relaxed somewhat, and betimes the prisoners would be seen taking a stroll of a summer's evening. The prisoners got to know the farm and the farmer's family very well as time passed, and they would take their midday meals with the family in the farmhouse, and so on.

One man of note, namely Antonio Travilioni (Tony for short), worked at Yew Tree Farm, the farmer at that time being Mr. Watkins. They were a most Christian family, and Tony enjoyed his time at Yew Tree such that, upon the cessation of hostilities, he sent for his wife and family of two girls, and they took tenancy of one of the new council houses in Perry Lane. Tony stayed on at Yew Tree until the Watkins family moved on, and thereafter he went to Wolverton railway works. Tony and his wife worked endlessly to improve their lot, and finally were able to buy the big house and acre of land opposite Harriets End. It followed that, with the smallholding, they were very happy with their life. His wife was a familiar sight walking down to the shop with her black pinafore full with peas in the pod, all grown in the garden with other produce in the season, but after a year or so she died suddenly, and so Tony sold up and took a smaller place in Newport.

By this time, the prison camp had been converted into temporary accommodation for those on the waiting list for council housing, and following that, it was a hostel for European voluntary workers. It was during the sixties that the site became available for building and known as Hillview. Forty years later, through the medium of the Rotary International Convention, one former prisoner, namely Pietro Gailiano from Reggio Emilia, came into the White Hart and was hoping to meet any old acquaintances, but memories had dimmed, although he did remember quite well Dick Middleweek, a solid Sheringtonian, who spent his life in a wheelchair. Dick and he spent a very pleasant hour together, and that was rewarding for them both. Once back in civilian life, Pietro took up his former profession as a goldsmith and silversmith. He started an apprentice school and was made a commendatore for his community work.

Earlier reference to the 1939/45 War recalls the measures that we, as a village, formed our own resistance to the Third Reich. Soon after the declaration, there appeared on the Knoll a large wooden hut, in fact it was a henhouse. It stood on four iron wheels, one on each corner, and was towable. It was situated next to the phone box, the reason being that the telephone from the kiosk could be used for the 'Fire Hut', as one could easily hear the phone ringing from the hut. The firefighting force was made up from men of the village. One remembers Messrs. Cliff Clare, Mick Hockenhull, Tom Umney, George Fleet, Charlie West, Frank Inns and Alan Johnson. They all done a duty, and someone was on call each and every night. It worked on a shift system. Inside the hut it was quite cosy and warm. Of course, they made endless cups of tea and often there were other beverages. Those firemen on duty were not the only occupants ... oh no ... many others called in as well. We had our own police force; Messrs. Sergeant Frank Howson, Fred Field, Harry Chappill, Jack Rose and Jack Cook. They had no such nerve centre, so they readily adopted an hour or so in the hut, as did the A.R.P. (Air Raid Precautions).

The Home Guard

At the formation of the fire service also came the Local Defence Volunteers (LDV), later called the Home Guard. The LDV had no

Sherington Home Guard

Back row from left: Albert Bailey, Charlie Peach, Frank Sedgewick, 'Kruschen' Austin
Front row from left: Fred Slater, Harry Loxley, Tom Goodman, Tom King, Joe Lane

uniform and carried their own shotguns. They filled a gap until we later had the uniformed Home Guard. The only meeting place for the LDV was a bell tent on top of Chicheley Hill, where the mound now stands. When erected by the bigger boys of Sherington School, it was a white canvas, but Headmaster Harold Bennet Kitchen ordered the boys to camouflage it and daub it with green paint, and that they did with a vengeance. The tent lasted a while until the small cottage on the Newport side of the Manor gates was taken over, and that, of course, was far more acceptable, one of the main reasons was the fireplace whereby they had warmth and could boil the kettle. Again, the special police force of Sherington availed themselves of the facility. It will be seen that there was always someone about during the hours of darkness, which was a reassurance to some with the village having no visible outside lighting. It is said that somehow the German Führer learned of Sherington's amalgamated defence force, and so fearful and apprehensive was Adolf Hitler, that he immediately strengthened the

German force. But to be serious for a minute, there is no doubt that these various combined forces would have proven to be a considerable hindrance to any advancing adversary, had the need arisen. The post-war scriptwriters have all had their fun and satire, and it can't be denied that there has been a very keen likeness from some of our members to those of Dad's Army. As a postscript, there were far too many members of the Home Guard to be mentioned here.

Organists

During the writing of these notes, mention was made of the list of organists at St. Laud's over the years and our memory goes back to Miss Elsie Line, who lived with her sister and parents in Park Road, holding that post for some time during the thirties. When she left to get married, Alfred Coverley of Newport took over. Alfie was most short in stature; he being four foot something, the organ had to be adjusted for his use of the pedal board. He was a likeable chap and very kind to the choirboys of the day. He was succeeded by Mrs. Flossie Jones, a village lady who

St. Laud's church choir with Rev. John Corfield in the 1970s

was a person of outstanding character. Mrs. Jones found it difficult to get on with the rector, Doggy Gordon, so she took the organist post at Emberton church. Doggy then invited 17-year-old Gerald Stratton from Newport to fill the post, which this up-and-coming organist accepted, the salary being twenty pounds a year for two services every Sunday, with choir practice added. Gerald continued until he joined the R.A.F., and then Johnny Warren, he also from Newport, filled in, and upon Gerald's demob, he resumed, by which time Doggy had left, and the living was taken jointly with Emberton under the Reverend H. I. K. Jones. Time went by, and when Gerald and Nina married, he left St. Laud's, and Flossie Jones returned. She held the post for a long time then, and in summing up her service to Sherington church, it was reckoned she had done forty years, and whilst we must not in any way be critical of Flossie, Nick Read came in as a breath of fresh air. He had trained at Newport under the tutorship of Mrs. Ethel Wesley, resident organist at Newport for many years. Under Nick, the choir at St. Laud's had eighteen members with some waiting out. They were young singers, and happiness reigned amongst them. Nick was invited to the organist post at Newport, and it was an offer he couldn't refuse, for it was a much better organ and the salary was higher, and, of course, it was his native town church. Nick was followed by John Hardcastle, who stayed awhile, then came Stephen Chilvers, who lived in Cranfield. Stephen stayed for nearly two years and went on to Olney. He was followed by Edwin Lack (from Newport), who stayed a long time and combined the SCAN (Sherington, Chicheley, Astwood with Hardmead and North Crawley) group of singers into the SCAN choir. Ed died quite suddenly to the sadness of us all, and he was to be followed by Robert Lawrence, who is still at St. Laud's.

Footpaths

When, in September 2010, the Thumbsticks 'beat the bounds' of Sherington, many questions were asked of the boundaries and the footpaths, rights of way, etc. Of footpaths, there are several, all of which are adequately signed. The most used in ages past must be the footpath alongside the flats in the High Street, passing through 'Longfield', it crosses Mill Lane and passes close by Charlesberry Kennels and out to the main highway at Sherington Bridge. By then, of course, you are halfway to Newport Pagnell, a market town much in demand in yesteryear. The footpath up Perry Lane and onwards takes one up to Bedlam Spinney, past Grange Farm and Thickthorn (a journey Sherington postmen did every day). It will be seen that those who walked to Bedford cut off quite a piece of the mileage by using that route.

Moving on to Water Lane, at the end of which the public highway runs onto the bridleway, that takes one on to End Farm and continues down to the kissing gate and leaves Sherington parish and enters the parish of Tyringham. The path goes on to their parish church. Should the reader leave the White Hart and walk down Gun Lane, on meeting the main Sherington to Olney road, walk straight across into 'Prices'; that walk will bring you to a mini-crossroads, whereupon one can turn right alongside Rectory Spinney and join the Filgrave road, or go straight ahead, passing Bakers Spinney, and by following the riding round, come out on the road leading to Fences Farm, and by following that, will come out close by Tyringham church. Should one wish to go in the Chicheley direction, then walk up Crofts End and take the footpath opposite the bungalows and come out opposite Sherington Nurseries,

Thumbsticks, Boxing Day walk, circa. 1977/78

and take the riding alongside the glasshouses known as Stocking Lane and proceed up the hill, and then take great care when crossing the by-pass, continuing on past the spinney, coming out at the top of Bedlam Lane, going down to the Chester Arms. The walks described are the principal walks in the village and will give the walker much pleasure. It should be emphasised that the walker ought not to divert from the routes aforementioned, particularly with dogs, unless one has the full permission of the landowner. Please note that it is the experience of those who ask, permission is rarely refused, and the Thumbsticks will certainly give endorsement to that. Before the advent of the motor car, country folk would walk many miles to their work or to visit relatives etc., with ten or a dozen miles being a 'mere bagatelle' to many. We should also take into account that most of our walking these days is for pleasure, and should the weather turn adverse then we don't bother, but the ordinary farm worker and the delivery man and so on had to go out whatever the weather, and often they would be cold and wet at the beginning of the day, only to remain so until the day's end.

Teddy Griffin

One mustn't overlook those people who were not professional, but possessed the knack of efficiency that the average person didn't need, and that calls to mind Teddy Griffin, a village man who lived a very simple life and who in his later years walked badly, such that he found other means of mobility in the form of a full-sized tricycle. 'Twas a robust affair with lever brakes and 28 inch wheels, Brooks saddle and battery lighting; altogether a most solid machine. Teddy could quite well manage to cycle to any local village, and was a regular sight on his way to Newport and back. His progress wasn't of high proportions, but he got there eventually, and, of course, he couldn't fall off. One summer's evening a group of village lads, those in their late teens, were pulling old Ted's leg, and after a while one of them, without Ted's blessing, got on the trike and went to make off with it, but he backed a loser 'cos he couldn't steer it or control it in any way. He was caught right off balance, and a right fool he made of himself with Ted standing smiling in the background.

Yet one more local skill, riding a trike, but not for everyone. Teddy Griffin had other strings to his bow. He was the only man known locally to jump off the parapet of Tyringham Bridge into the water below, and after coming out onto the bank, would dry him on a canvas corn sack, a method he maintained would help the blood circulation. Teddy was single for most of his life, but in his closing years he made friends with 'Gran' Watts, and so, he being 79 years old and Gran being 81 years old, they married in the Wesleyan chapel on the Knoll and lived happily ever after.

Wedding of Teddy Griffin and 'Gran' Watts in the 1950s

Ben Line

Ben Line mustn't be left out of those talented village craftsmen who seemed to be 'jack of all trades'. He was the organist for over 40 years at the Congregational chapel in Calves End. The organ there was called an American organ, probably known as a harmonium, a two-pedal job with knee swells. It was surprising what results came from that instrument, and it was certainly adequate for all demands in that building. Ben was the village barber. Most evenings after tea he would be seen with his

Ben Line

Gladstone bag bearing tools of trade, keeping his regular appointments which, after he had finished, came the cups of tea and the bit of supper and a bigger bit of gossip, and oft-times it would be quite late as he closed the garden gate. He had yet one more sideline, that of chimney sweep. It was said he was one of the tidiest in that trade and always carried a hand brush etc. to clean up after he had done the dirty work. Never in a hurry, he always had time to stop and tell you a story of some sort, and the job in hand often came second to that, but Ben Line was a fine Englishman, the like of which we shall rarely see again.

Jack Pateman

Much could be written of the skills and talents possessed by the residents of the village, some of them reaching unknown depths and measures. Take, for instance, our village roadman, Jack Pateman, who was unable to read or write, or even to tell the time of day, and yet he

Jack Pateman, with his wife, Amy, in the Swan

was without compare even in his occupation as a roadman. It seemed he had a forewarning of the weather at all times of the year. At the beginning of any new year he was on 'red alert' with his wheelbarrow and shovel, spreading the sand on the road surface and following on to the footpaths all round. Come the April showers and heavy storms, out came the heavy waterproofs and waders, ready to unblock the ditches and water courses, drains and whatever. All this, of course, led one into the early summer, thus with it came the grass cutting and mowing. Ah, how well remembered is he with his scythe, standing it on end with the blade held up high that he could sharpen it with his 'wet stone'. How, with an exact rhythm, he wiped the sharpening stone across the blade, and smiling he would say, "You could shave your face with that", and it was no idle boast. After he had mown the Knoll, it would be of lawnmower standard, very much welcomed by the young children who regularly played there long years before the village hall play area was created.

Kit Clare

Kit Clare, well-known village character, was oft-times seen helping out behind the bar in the Swan, but her principal role for many years in Sherington and district was the village milkmaid. Working for our dairyman, namely George Fleet of Village Farm, she delivered the milk to the doorstep of most houses here, and her raucous voice

Kit Clare (right), with Pat Major, landlady of the Swan one time

could be heard most strongly if things weren't going her way. Carrying out her duties through storm and tempest, fair weather and foul, she

The presentation to George Fleet and Kit Clare on their retirement - taken on Mayday, it also shows the Mayday queen and her attendants of the day

could wrap her tongue round a swear word or two, but never ever an obscenity. Born of farming stock and sister to Mrs. Ted Duncombe of the Chicheley Farming dynasty, Kit was a country girl throughout. She lived in the cottage on the Knoll with her husband Jim Clare of the well-known Clare family, antique dealers etc. of Newport Pagnell.

It was said she always called a spade a spade. It could also be said she called it everything else as well, but such was the way of this lovable lady, who could always find time and room for just one afore ye go. Happy memories of Kit Clare and her family will linger long hereabouts.

Trees on the Knoll

At that time there were no trees on the Knoll. The big London plane tree just behind the bus shelter was planted by Mrs. Wellesley Taylor of Sherington Manor, very much a local dignitary. It was planted in celebration of the Silver Jubilee in the reign of King George V and Queen Mary in May 1935. As young village boys, it is well remembered 'cos when the lady of the Manor planted the tree she threw into the hole

Tree planting by Mrs. Doris Clutton on the Knoll in 1937

a lucky shilling with great ceremony, and 'Shanny' Line calling out, "Let me get it out." Some two years later, another tree was planted by Mrs. Wellesley Taylor's daughter, namely Mrs. Doris Clutton, who was the wife of Lt. Col. John Clutton, retired. The said tree was planted up at the far end of the Knoll, but it didn't survive for long, one reason given was that it was poisoned or destroyed with salt water by the Lathbury gents who schooled privately at Knoll Cottage, but that's another story.

Thatching

Old Long Un keeps turning up in these readings, and so he should, for he was a man of many talents. Thatching was his main occupation and his busy time was in the late summer and autumn when the hay time and harvest was done. Each farmer would try to get his haystacks and cornstalks up in the rickyard within the farmyard proper, but on occasion they would build a rick down the field for feeding convenience. Long Un had as his workmate and helper, Harry Line, a member of a well-known and respected Sherington family. Harry had been a time-serving soldier, much of his time spent in India. What a change for the ex-service man to be thatching a hay rick after having done his time in the Punjab. The pair had all the right equipment – three ladders of various lengths, the knives and the big ball of string, and, of course, the

Mrs. Tatham's house and thatch that Long Un kept in order

hazel or willow spits that served as pegs to hold down the thatch in the storms. And always the wheelbarrow, and, you may ask, what had that to do with thatching? The barrow was to take the one-hundredweight iron block that was roped to the bottom rung of the ladder, so that the ladder didn't slip whilst they were up aloft. There were quite a number of thatched houses and barns in the village then-a-day, and the two workmen would have enough to see them through till rick building time came round

Thatching Miss McKenzie's home in Church Road, 1920s

again. These men had neither office nor accounting system. They kept no records, only within their memory, but they knew their clients and knew who was next on the list and when they would pay their annual visit, each farmer in his turn. Whatever the weather, storm or tempest, the crop beneath the thatched roof would be perfectly dry throughout and therein laid the skill of the thatcher man.

Artists

It is always interesting to look over the work of past artists, who were residents of the village, and, therefore, had a good insight of the subjects they put on their canvas or boards. Sherington has been rich in such skills, certainly for the last hundred years or more. Edith Lucas dated most of her work, and that goes back to the 1890s through the early 1900s. A farmer's daughter, Edith lived with her family at Bakers Farm in Olney Road, and it was her who bequeathed a collection of paintings to the village, prints of which are to be seen in the village hall as this is written.

Bakers Farm by Edith Lucas, painted in 1894

Painting of a hunting scene by Tom Ivester Lloyd

Following Miss Lucas was Tom Ivester Lloyd, a much more professional artist and nationally known. Specialising in equestrian and hunting scenes, he was acknowledged as a leader in horse and hound illustration and was published regularly in field and sporting magazines. His son, Jack Ivester Lloyd, was equally well known as a sporting journalist, and so they complimented each other very well in their work. It was in Tom Lloyd's time that 'Ole Crump' appeared, and he wasn't old at all. Arthur Crump, known locally as Charlie, was of middle- to upper-class stock and schooled in London. He was a member of the Royal Institute of Oil Painters and had a studio in Stoke Newington, where, apparently, he lived. Much of his early work was done in the rurality of Kent and where his work was hung at exhibitions. The subjects were mainly of Kentish character. Crump suffered a mental breakdown whilst copying a master in a leading London gallery, and, we are told, attacked the master in his malady. As a result, he learned of a farmhouse in Buckinghamshire that took in paying guests, and he was advised to take a rest away from the metropolis and come to Sherington. The house in question was Home Farm, where Doctor and Mrs. Jenny Skinner now live, and the occupants were Mr. Henry and Mrs. Gardner, the late Peter Gardner's grandparents. Crump was due to stay for two weeks, after which time he was collected and went back to London, but he yearned to return to Home Farm, and so his family brought him back, where he stayed much longer. Their attempt to get him to return to London met with a refusal, and so, in the interest of health, he stayed here and then started once more in his artistry. Folklore has it that he was visited by his family in their fine limousine, and repeatedly they asked him to go back to London, but that was not to be, and he continued his domicile here in Sherington.

The elderly couple, Mr. and Mrs. Gardner, passed from this world and Crump moved into the big house on the Knoll now under the ownership of Mr. and Mrs. Tony Pilcher; the occupants at that time being Mr. Harry and Mrs. Elizabeth West. Crump could be seen in and about the district and was becoming well known, not only for his art, but for his eccentricity also. He became unkempt, had a long beard, wore the same

Arthur Crump's painting of the High Street, circa. 1920s

Sherington High Street today from the same location as Crump's painting above

trilby hat, raincoat and wellingtons at all times. Apparently, he loved the ladies and would do a sketch of a pretty girl at the drop of a hat. As time went by, for whatever reason, he became poverty stricken and would resort to drawing on the cardboard of a writing pad, evidence of which this writer is in possession. Crump became more and more odd and would talk to himself constantly and destroyed much of his work in a fit of temper or exasperation. In his closing days he was causing concern to Mr. and Mrs. West, who were now quite aged and had a job to do for themselves, and so it was, the medical profession concluded, he was not of sound mind, and he was taken from the Knoll on a Saturday afternoon. He putting up a good physical resistance, and very much to the dismay of the elder ladies of the village, who had, in their way, become quite fond of Arthur Crump, many of them calling out to those who were taking him away that they should be ashamed. And so Arthur Crump went away to Stone, near Aylesbury, the local lunatic asylum then called, where he died. He was buried here in St. Laud's churchyard, the gravesite unknown, but his work and his memory lives on; a brilliant artist and one to whom, with every credit, the Sherington Historical Society has done much to recognise.

During the 1930s, the family Fielder moved into number eight Council Houses, Church Road, then opposite the village hall. Mr. Montague Fielder was an artist, not only with brush and pallet, but musically equally. He was something of the last of the bohemian, never seen without a bow tie, hand tied and invariably with a carnation buttonhole. There is still one or two of his paintings hanging in homes in the village. He also played a one-string violin, fitted with a small horn to produce more sound. Montague Fielder might still be remembered by some playing his violin, accompanied by his wife on the mini-piano, in the best room in the Crown and Castle of a Saturday night, playing some of the classics of the day, but more than anything he was a fine artist.

Some years later came Paul Mann, who lived in Calgary House in Church End. He had adopted a revolutionary method of art. He used cellulose paint for some of his work, applied more with a pallete knife

Paul Mann standing by his painting in the village hall

than brush. Paul was an 'artiste internationale', and his work is hung throughout the country. He moved, with his wife Olga, to Lincolnshire in the late 70s.

To date, we have resident here Martin Williams, a professional artist of international reputation, whose exhibitions, both in the provinces and the City of London are always well patronised. In recent times, Martin travelled to Hong Kong to fulfil a commission. He and his family live in Church Road. His painting of the author features on the back cover of this book.

We must not finish without mention of Caroline Leslie, a lady who has willingly obliged all requests for her skills as an illustrator and artist. During her career, she worked for a leading magazine publisher, thus her work was very well recognised. She lives with her family in Calves End. She has painted the front cover for this book, and see her drawings of the mound on page 92.

*Norman Arnold's Clock Shop, Sherington painted by John Kitchen Snr.
in July 1987 for Norman's 60th birthday*

*Fire at No. 12 High Street, Sherington, 1962 – painting by John Kitchen
Jnr., 1992*

Nor must we omit our former headmaster of Sherington school, Charles Stephens. His life was dedicated to teaching, but his pastime was painting, and he gave his skills to notelets and such, that they could be sold in aid of charity, mainly for St Laud's, of which he was for many years churchwarden (see his drawing on page 14).

In conclusion, how dare we miss out John Kitchen Snr. whose work hangs on many a front room and lounge wall. Famous for his infectious smile and for his Sherlock Holmes' pipe; old JK didn't waste his time or keep his talents to himself, 'cos his son John Kitchen Jnr. is highly thought of in his work; he being a master of producing cartoons, that doesn't lessen his reputation in serious art.

This chapter has by no means recorded all the artists in this village over the years, but has touched on some whose work can still be seen today.

Timber Merchants

The man who wanted the shilling out of the hole at the planting of the Jubilee tree, namely Shanny Line, worked for his namesake, John Line and Sons, timber merchants, whose yard and sawmill was in Church Road. John Line was a one-time foreman of the timber department of Messrs. Salmons and Sons, the famous coachbuilders of Newport Pagnell. Always wanting to run his own business, he started in a very small way, cutting fencing rails and posts etc., and gradually built up his business through hard work and careful spending. He bought most of his timber, what they called 'standing'. That meant, as it had grown, therefore he had to fell all that he bought.

The workforce being John Line, his sons Bill and Ben and Shanny. They had a horse-drawn timber carriage and all the necessary tools and tackle to do the job right, all the tools being hand powered. The cross-cut saw, for actually cutting through the tree trunk, was six foot long with a handle at each end, so with a man on each of the handles, it was a push-and-pull action that made the cut. Each man kneeling on a bag of sawdust, they soon got into a rhythm and would make the cut through without stopping, the whole tree falling to the ground in thereabouts the given spot. Rarely were they above an inch or two from the predicted line of fall. The fellers would have, what they called, a short blow, which meant a minute or so rest and then set about the trimming of the head. Firstly, dealing with the small twigs and foliage, they would then sever the thicker limbs and put them carefully into 'cords'. A cord of wood hereabouts was a careful measure, and this is what they done ... drive a round stake into the ground nearby, leaving four feet above the ground, measure four feet distance from that stake, and drive another into the ground likewise. Now you have two stakes four feet apart and both four foot high. Next, measure an eight-foot length from the two stakes and drive two stakes into the ground aforesaid. You should now have four stakes in the ground, measuring eight by four on the ground and four foot high. Now the tree feller cuts all his trimmings to four foot long, stacks them tidily between the stakes, and when finished he should have a stack of cut trimmings 8 x 4 x 4. That is a cord of wood, and many a woodman will have stacked many a cord. Then, of course, they are sold off, the buyer giving so much a cord, each cord going to firewood, the sale of which would help towards the wages bill. In the woodyard was the big rack bench whereupon the main tree trunk was rolled. It was a

Line and Sons' timber yard

The timber yard: John Line and his sons, Bill and Ben, with Spot the dog, 1925

Derelict sheds in Line's timber yard

very long bench that would easily take the length of the trunk, going backwards and forwards on rollers, slicing the boards about an inch thick, they being carefully stacked alongside. Many of the trees were elm – this part of the country being rich in that variety – the converted timber being mainly used for coffin boards, of which there was a healthy demand. Of course, there was always the resultant sawdust that stood in a very high heap in the yard, where the villagers would come with their bags and use it for whatever purpose, paying a few pence a bag for it.

The Marshall single-cylinder steam engine would be heard, as aforementioned, puffing away with its rhythmical song, accompanied by the whine of the big circular saw digging its teeth into the resisting tree. The whole operation was one of physical demand as much as anything, and it was surprising how they managed to produce in the way they did with so little mechanical assistance. One of Sherington's most important industries in the years leading up to the 39/45 War, it faded out when John Line's two sons, Bill and Ben, were conscripted into the armed forces. When they returned to civilian life, the sawmill and the steam engine had fallen into disrepair, and even if it had been operational, the business had by now fallen behind the times, and their equipment was outdated. John Line was by now quite aged, so the boys turned their hand to local and jobbing building, and the woodyard was silenced; old 'Puffing Billy' never to be heard again.

The timber carriage, a four-wheeled, skeleton-framed affair, was drawn by a shire horse of immense power. John Line had three such horses in the stable, all of which earned their keep. They drew the timber from any of the outlying villages in this area, thus there were some heavy work on the ups and downs of the rolling countryside where the trees were felled. Of course, the horses were treated with great affection and were spoken to as if they were human. The horse keeper would often talk to the horse were there no one other to relate. It was well known that out in the countryside horses were power, and as a result they were respected. They all had a name, and as boys it is remembered the number of tradesmen and deliverymen whose vehicles were horse drawn. The heavy horses of

John Line's timber yard worked jolly hard, but there were others who had a much lighter load, such as the butcher and baker.

Horses

One well-known Sheringtonian was Reg Watts, who drove the coal cart for Francis Coales and Son of Newport Pagnell. A most popular man, Reg would be seen with his four-wheeled trolley in all the villages round, and his horse's name was Gertie. Many are the apples and biscuits and sweets that Gertie received on the round. She certainly had many friends who would listen for the clippety-clop approaching, and out they would go to pat the neck and stroke the nose, a cold drink being most welcome on a mildish morning, the housewife holding the bucket awhile. Reg Watts left the coalyard in Station Road with the trolley fully loaded with twenty-five bags of coal, and he would deliver five or so in the town, so that Gertie didn't pull the full load out to the villages. He is well remembered negotiating the downhill from North Square to Mill Street on a frosty and snowy morning with his eagerly awaited winter fuel. On such occasions, the horse's shoes were fitted with spikes to prevent slipping. Of course, there were many other horse-drawn carts. Every morning throughout the year, the milk float left Yew Tree Farm in this village for Newport, where all morning was spent delivering to many households, the vendor carrying a three-gallon can, with the two measurer hanging within, half pint and full pint, it being poured into the householder's jug on the doorstep. It would be after dinner time when the farmer and his daughter could be seen trotting back home, having given a service that started quite early in the morning with the bringing in the cows, and then the hand milking and cooling and pouring it into the big churns and loading it into the float and onward trotting into town to make the first of many calls.

Back at the farm, there were the heavier work horses; fine sixteen and seventeen hands they stood, a near on ton of muscle on four legs. Lovely names – Whitefoot, Captain and Bonny come to mind. The horse that pulled the float was named Gypsy and was regarded at Yew Tree Farm as one of the family. Gypsy had an almost human understanding of the daily routine and would stop at each delivery point without guidance or control. Because of her daily road work, her shoes needed attention quite regularly, and it followed that a visit to the well-known blacksmith in Newport, Mr. Jack Bailey, was called for. Jack was a most genial man who, with his wife Mabel, kept the Dolphin on Market Hill. The second man at the 'Smithy' and equal in his skills was Bill Bishop, who was under the employ of Jack Bailey, both of whom would allow, from time to time, a young schoolboy to pump the bellows of the forge and make the flames roar, but we should go back once more to Gypsy just to say that, on completion of the town milk round, the last stop was North Square where the farmer's daughter then delivered that area, whilst the farmer would visit the Neptune public house and partake thereof the victuals. The story goes that one Christmas morning in the High Street in Newport a wandering musician, homeless and destitute,

was playing Christmas music on the piccolo, and such was his plight, cold and without warmth, the farmer took his overcoat off and handed it to the journeyman, who moved on much more comfortable that Christmas Day, and the farmer drove back to Sherington with Gypsy, less his topcoat and not so warm as his outward trip. They were creatures of habit, the menfolk of Yew Tree Farm, and each year, for many years, they would borrow the neighbour's long ladder when rick building. One year in particular, the farmer sent his

Johnny, the cart horse, circa. 1950, led by Wilf Rollinson

brother, Frank, to borrow the ladder, but for the first time ever the neighbour wouldn't loan, for diverse reasons. Well now, their world collapsed. "You what?" said the farmer, "We can't have it? What on earth shall we do?" Needless to say, they recovered from that dreadful experience.

Just down the road from Yew Tree Farm, old Tommy Pharaoh, who was a horse dealer and always went about in a 'fly', a light, two-wheeled passenger float with high wheels, and with a 'high stepper' in the shafts was capable of quite fast travel. Ole bearded Tommy would always find a job for the odd-job man, just to give him a chance to earn a shilling. A high stepper being a half-legged horse, very fast trotter and one that lifted its legs up high when doing so. Up at Church Farm they had Johnny, a heavy horse who could do his job well and wasn't afraid of a day's work, such was his reputation that other farmers would often borrow him. They certainly did at Yew Tree. Down at Water Lane, Mr. George West ran a smallholding, whilst his wife ran what is known as Virginia House Stores. He had a biggish pony named Peggy, and she done the milk round too. Alongside Peggy there was another in the stable, but a much more majestic figure; a First War 1914/1918 veteran with its army number tattooed in its mouth in the bottom gum. Called Depper, one First War villager explained that he would have been a depot horse, and Depper is a corruption of that. We boys remember Depper very well as a calm, powerful, friendly horse, of which we had great affection. Nearby at Water Lane Farm, Mr. Dudley Gardner kept Big Ben, seventeen or over hands, a real big shire horse that had trouble getting under the stable door. As some say, those were the days, and so they were for those of a slower way of life, but the motor car was taking over, and with petrol at 1/9d per gallon at Haynes' garage, one could travel a long way for a pound, because 1/9d converted equals 9 new pence of today's reading. Thus 9 new pence for 5 litres!

Building of the Motorway

Over fifty years after the M1 motorway was built, the Sherington Historical Society received an enquiry from the University of Westminster, searching for information about the labour force employed on that project, and were any accommodated in Sherington? The answer to that enquiry is certainly 'Yes'. The main contractor for the motorway project hereabouts was John Laing of London, and their outriders came to Sherington just before work started and secured the tenancy of the former prisoner of war camp in Perry Lane (now Hillview), following which some 40 to 50 caravans were parked for the duration of the contract, and very comfortable homes they were. The occupants were clearly accustomed to living that way of life, moving wherever their work was located. The families were seen daily in the shops and taking the children to school just the same as the permanent residents. Many

Opening of the M1 motorway, November 1959

of the employees held high positions within the company and were to be seen leaving their homes immaculately dressed with their briefcases in hand. The resident engineer, who was in sole command on the site, lived in lodgings in Park Road and used the White Hart as his local; as a consequence, many sought his company in that place. The financial director lived in the High Street, next but one to the then village shop, and so Sherington saw many skilled engineers within the parish bounds during the course of the motorway construction. The demand for gravel aggregates were excessive, as one could imagine, thus one hundred acres of meadowland in Emberton were opened up for mineral deposits, with dozens of lorries daily passing through Sherington en route to the various sections of the operation. Meanwhile, along the Newport Road, Messrs. Hartigan was under great demand for their products, and many of the fishing lakes we see today are the result of their gravel diggings. The motorway brought prosperity to hoteliers, bed and breakfast homes, public houses and shops, and all sorts of entrepreneurs, and the heavy traffic that once groaned its way from and to London and the north country, all passing over Newport's iron bridge and High Street, were seen no more for better or for worse.

It was some years later that Newport Pagnell rural district council purchased the abandoned gravel workings at Emberton, they being spent of all gravel anyway, and so from the brutal assault of the diggers and the general upheaval of the meadowland, the Ouse Valley at Emberton came the pleasure park that we see today: out of turmoil comes peace and quiet in the fullness of time.

SCAN

Oft on the tongue nowadays is, "We must put something in SCAN", which is the title of our monthly magazine. SCAN is taken from the first letter of the villages in the rector's living, thus Sherington, Chicheley, Astwood with Hardmead and North Crawley, and it was about that time under a diocesan order the five parishes and livings were grouped together under the leadership of the Reverend Leslie Bearman, the then incumbent and resident in Sherington rectory. He first published a plain single broadsheet news-sheet, and distributed it round the villages in order to keep the residents abreast of church news. At that time, it was done on a Roneo copier, a sort of 'wind the handle' job supervised and operated by Mrs. Sheila Minet of that time resident in Chicheley old rectory. The publication took off readily, and people looked forward to SCAN and all was well. After a time, Reverend Bearman retired, and his successor was the Reverend John Corfield, who was keenly interested in SCAN, which had by now taken a folded book form with a masthead and it was dated each month. It will be realised that the Roneo equipment was inadequate for the purpose, and so John Burgess, a local businessman, took on the printing and collating, with volunteer distributors covering the villages. Each village by now had their own correspondent, and all the local news was fed into the rectory office. There was a period when, between the changes from the Roneo to John Burgess, the Reverend Corfield called for assistance of the late David Pinder and another local helper. They both agreed to go out within the catchment area and sell advertising, a scheme that brought in enough revenue to honour all debts. As aforementioned, John Burgess took over, and that lasted a long time, but SCAN by now was becoming ever demanding in time, so John handed over the printing to Henry

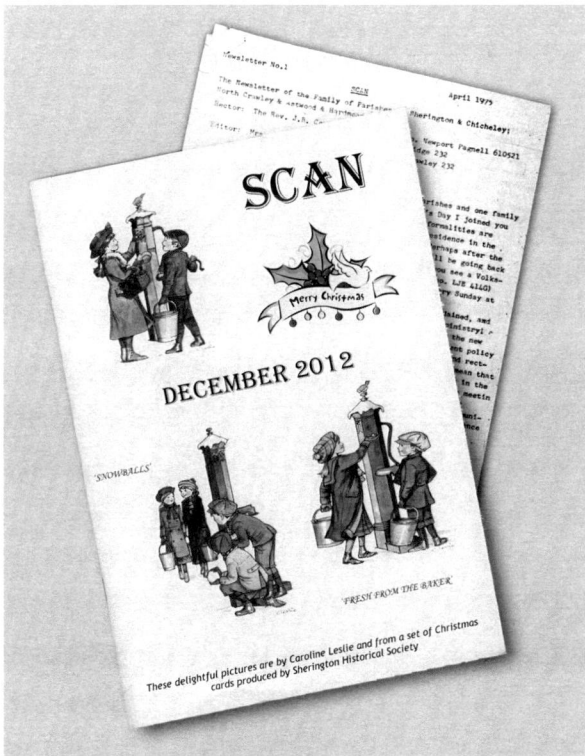

The first SCAN and one of the most recent, which features Caroline Leslie's Christmas designs on the front cover

Powell-Shedden, who had an accountancy business in Newport Pagnell. By now, many other helpers had built SCAN magazine into more of a parish magazine, and the church no longer held any responsibility for its running, and thus it was not a church magazine, the whole administration and management being completely free from all others. Quite a few changes were made in editorship; Mrs. Pam Haynes, Mrs. Harriet Milner and currently Mrs. Betty Feasey; with Mr. Philip Smith standing in when needed, providing continuity and invaluable advice alongside writing his 'Little Bird' column for many years. The duties of treasurer and advertising manager were also taken on by a succession of willing volunteers, ensuring the 'books' were kept in order. Only once during its lifetime has an appeal for money been made on its behalf, when a small brown envelope was attached to each copy, and the result was in the region of £500. Financially it is self-supporting through advertising revenue and donations. Many people deserve much credit for the long life of SCAN magazine, but were they all to be mentioned, then that would be a mammoth task.

Toffees

If there was any pleasure in going to school in Sherington, and some would say they were few, although many of us were happy and content enough, one bonus was Mrs. Nursaw's toffees. The lady lived in the house next to the school (the old school that is) known as Laundry Cottage. They did at one time do the laundry there for the church and the rector. Mrs. Nursaw made her toffee each school day in a large tray, the squares measuring about an inch apiece, marked out with a knife. There were but two nominations to purchase, a ha'p'orth or a pen'orth; a ha'p'orth would be served in a small, triangular-shaped bag, about the size of an ice cream cone, containing about half-a-dozen toffees. The pen'orth served in a square bag with a dozen within. Naturally, the ha'p'orth was the popular sale in that it was the cheaper. The daily pattern of this school-day ritual was only broken during the late summer, when the apple harvest was at its best and the dear lady made toffee apples, but of course they were a penny apiece, so very often they would be

The Nursaws outside Laundry Cottage

purchased on a shared basis – one bite in turn till only the stick was left. When one boy asked if he could have the core he was told that, "There ain't no core". Mrs. Nursaw was held in the greatest respect by both young and old, a really lovely lady, who never saw ill in any of the schoolchildren, but understood the poverty within the families of the village, and in her way she relieved that economical way of life for some by making her famous toffees. The money raised, she always gave in full to the Congregational chapel in Calves End, of which her husband was a senior elder. Mrs. Nursaw, a lovely, happy, most-valued friend of all the children of that era and, of course, as already mentioned elsewhere, mother of eight daughters and a son.

SHEFCO

Talking of the past, during recent days the question was asked, "Who and what was this SHEFCO?" The short answer is that it is an abbreviation for the Sherington feast committee. They were a body of residents in the village, who, when the feasts were over and done with, still hungered for community work and entertainment, and who got together and did much worthwhile and necessary tasks; activities that were of benefit to us all. One pivotal member of the village was to say that it all came about with the advent of Milton Keynes, and his reasoning was that the new city brought a new life into villages such as ours, many of whom had previously had no taste of village life, liked what they saw and wanted to become involved in whatever was afoot. And so it was that many a freshman was recognised for his talents and skills, and coupled with the natives and the established members, they readily became of benefit to the community. Many of the events that were organised gave much pleasure and comfort and enjoyment to the residents. The outings to Chatsworth, Sandringham, Windsor and Margate; the sanding and varnishing of the village hall floor; the raising money for the church roof; the concreting of the ramp to enable the invalid lady and her husband to negotiate the access the better; and onward we could go.

And we must not pass without a mention of the sponsored 'bike rides'. The first was to a small hamlet in Wiltshire on the other side of Salisbury Plain, and the name of that hamlet was Sherrington. We got to know of it through our rector at that time, the Reverend John Corfield. He, with his wife Rachel, had stayed in their camper-van in the quiet of that hamlet overnight, and the next day, being Sunday, went to the small church there, and upon leaving, the rector there bid them greetings and enquired from whence they came. "From Sherington", came the reply. "Oh," said the resident minister, thinking they lived in his Sherrington, "And what do you do for a living?" "I'm the rector there", came the reply, and, of course, the usual banter was enjoyed. As a result of that encounter, SHEFCO decided to bike there. It is 120 miles each way, each family who entered the ride to do 10 miles apiece; thus 12 teams there, and the same teams to do 10 miles each on the return journey. They encamped in a nearby field overnight and immense fun and pleasure was had. Bill Norton, the landlord of the Swan, driving the beer wagon, and Peter Gardner filming all the way there and back. The money raised bought two beds for the then new Milton Keynes hospital in answer to an appeal for public support to get the hospital under way. The next bike ride was to Terrington in Norfolk, a village

Home at last! Cheering participants at the finish of the sponsored bike ride from Sherington, Bucks. to Sherrington, Wilts. – 120 miles each way, a 2-day event

that the aforementioned Reverend John Corfield had moved on to. A similar exercise followed that of Sherrington, and again much money was raised and equal pleasure enjoyed. SHEFCO also entered Newport Pagnell Carnival with a view of taking first prize, and they did just that. SHEFCO members put their whole heart in all they did with no half measure. They are still talked of and still about, and they may yet again answer the calls or the demands of this parish, and who knows, there may be yet another Sherington feast.

Transport

There were not many motor cars in this village in the early thirties – only a dozen or so – Reverend Bloomfield and Mr. Dudley Gardner, Mr. Haynes, Mrs. Wellesley Taylor, Charlie Peach and Mr. Ern Fleet. All old-fashioned upright cars worth £25/30 apiece.

The method of travel was by bus, of which there was a fair choice. There was a family business, Mr. and Mrs. Gammons, who ran a service between Bedford and Oxford, calling at every village and town on the route. Their Dennis coach groaned its way through Bromham, Turvey, Lavendon, Olney, Emberton, Prospect, Sherington, and onward and forward. Leaving Bedford at 7 a.m., the coach would pass through Sherington at 8.15 a.m., through to Oxford, arriving there about 11 a.m. and would pass through here on its return trip to Bedford at 12.55 p.m., only to go back to Oxford at 3.15 p.m., and passing finally back to Bedford at 8 p.m. through Sherington. So you could go to Oxford in one from here. Mr. Gammon drove the coach, and his daughter Gwen was the conductress. In those days, many people caught 'The Oxford'.

Messrs. Hayfield of Newport ran the Northampton service with particular attention on Wednesday and Saturday, both of which were market days. Leaving Market Hill, Newport, the service ran through each and every village to Northampton, passing through Sherington, Filgrave and Tyringham on to Northampton. The other company, Messrs. Wesley of Stoke Goldington, ran the 'Picture Bus', a most important function, it catered for night owls. The service ran through Ravenstone, Weston Underwood, Olney, Emberton and on to the Electra Cinema at Newport for six days or nights of the week. Quite often it called for two coaches, 'cos not all the people went to the cinema; many would call at the various pubs or call on their relatives. A very important service was the Picture Bus.

Messrs. Souls of Olney also came into the reckoning. Why, at 9 a.m. of a Wednesday one could catch a coach on the Knoll that would take you to London, where it parked at the back of Oxford Street and stood there all day, thus you could go back to it whenever you liked with your purchases. The service brought you back here mid-evening. We mustn't leave out the National Network. Hereabouts we had the Eastern National Service, which provided a regular run twixt here and Bedford and Stony Stratford. An hourly service, it catered for the important Wolverton Works run etc. Always double- deckers, they operated come

Hayfield bus trip to Clacton, circa. 1920s

storm or tempest, rarely did they fail. If you had the stamina, you could take a trip to the seaside, but that, of course, is another story.

Thumbsticks

In Sherington village there are a number of very keen walkers, who can be seen walking the highways and byways of the district. They meet on a monthly basis, with one or two specials thrown in during the year. It all started some 35 to 40 years ago, when the walkers at that time wished to 'beat the bounds' of the parish. This they did, and much enjoyed the walk, and over the years it has been walked several, if not many, times. One or two of the menfolk, they were a mixed company, carried a thumbstick, and over the course of time, a few more were to be seen doing likewise, and so the name the 'Thumbsticks' came about. The leader would seek permission of the local landowners and tenant farmers to walk their land, and there were only one or two who declined. The footpaths in Sherington have been trodden many times over, and so it was found necessary to go into other parishes and enjoy their facilities. Over the years, it goes without saying, most of the earlier band have now retired or passed on, but there still can be seen a dozen or more of a Sunday morning meeting on the Knoll, awaiting the 'kick-off'. The longest day

The first Thumbsticks walkers, early 1970s

sees the start at an earlier time than the regular 9.30 a.m. from the Knoll, because on that morning, 21st June, they meet at 3.15 a.m. to see the darkness break into daylight, and it is, by definition, the most peaceful of all the walks. The other regular is the 'Searchlight' walk. It starts at a particular point on the road from Hardmead to Newton Blossomville on a notable dangerous bend on that road, during the war years posted there was a searchlight battery, its location being of a somewhat high point. The land is under the ownership of Andrew Finn-Kelcey Esq. of Clifton Pastures, a gentleman in every respect who annually gives permission to the Thumbsticks to pass over his land as it is not a public footpath. Each year, just before Advent, as the gentleman writes, on 'pudden in the pot' Sunday, meaning stir-up Sunday, the leader writes to the farmer and he writes back by return giving written permission. This ritual has gone on for many years, courtesies shown and respected by both parties, albeit, both farmer and leader being the best of friends for many, many years. The searchlight walk finishes at Emberton, where for the last twenty-five years or more the Thumbsticks have been entertained to breakfast at West Lane House, which is the residence of Alderman and Mrs. Caroline Ellis. How the breakfast came about was from an earlier invitation to stop and rest awhile at West Lane House and get your breath back, after something like a four-mile walk. 'Tis an annual breakfast that brings the feeling of approaching Christmastide and is now very much a part of the Thumbsticks Calendar. The home of the Ellis's is always most welcoming and greetings of the warmest. How fitting is the quotation from William Shakespeare – *The Taming of the Shrew* – which reads, 'Let them want nothing that my house affords'. In this essay, one or two people have been mentioned in particular, merely to give some idea of the good relations that the Thumbsticks enjoy locally, but it must be emphasised that both landowners and their tenants have given the Thumbsticks walking rights without reserve, a privilege that money couldn't buy, and it is known that there is a permanent gratitude for the concessions as mentioned.

What was that old song we learned at school ...

> *"Jog on, jog on, the footpath way*
> *So merrily hent the tiler*
> *A merry heart goes all the way*
> *A sad tires in a miler."*

The last Thumbsticks walk led by the author, February 2012 –
Thumbsticks carries on with a group of people taking it in turns to lead
the monthly walks

The Blue Bridge

Ever since the world began, one supposes, the River Great Ouse has flowed its way from the Oxfordshire border, across Bucks and Beds counties, through the Fen district and on to the Wash. We are told that the Great Ouse rises from a very small spring near the village of Greatworth, out there near Brackley, and ever increasing in volume, by the time it passes through north Bucks, 'tis something like 30 to 40 yards wide, varying in depth from 3 feet to 20 feet. In recent times, with the policy being larger land operations, small farms being no longer profitable, we have the situation whereby a landowner will hold land either side of the river and that 30 to 40 yard-wide stretch of water causing a very long detour to get from one side to another. Such was the case hereabout with Manor Farm, owning land both on the Sherington side and the Lathbury side, causing, give or take, a five-mile detour, should one take it to extreme. It followed that, having finished combining the field at Lathbury, then the combine with all its attendant equipment had to travel through Lathbury, along to the Woad Corner, along over Sherington Bridge into this village. Water Lane being too narrow, go up Olney road, through Bakers and on toward the river-side fields. One can see it was a very inconvenient and time-consuming journey, even more so all those years ago in horse and cart days. Modern farming has not time for such time-wasting, and so it was that the local landowner put on his thinking cap and designed a steel bridge that would span the river at a convenient spot; a bridge of 25 tons carrying capacity, and wide enough to take a combine of the largest magnitude. The bridge manufacture was entrusted to a Bedford engineering company, namely

Crane placing the Blue Bridge, August 1997

Various shots of the placing of the Blue Bridge, August 1997

C.A.E.C. Howard, under the personal direction of Brian Howard, a family member. Transported in sections and assembled on site, it was lifted in one piece by the largest crane hereabouts, and when lowered into position, the anchor bolts fitted perfectly with exact precision. The landowner, who conceived the whole exercise, was the first to step up on to the bridge and to walk from one side of the River Great Ouse to the other without getting his feet wet. When the necessary banking and ramping was complete a few days later, young Michael Haynes, of the Haynes Engineering family, drove the massive combine over the new bridge with only inches to spare, only to be followed by David Turner with the second one, thus linking Lathbury with Sherington by means of the 'Blue Bridge'. It must be added that the River Board were consulted in every particular. The bridge was erected on 14th August 1997.

Readers should note: there is no right of way over the bridge, but walkers are usually welcomed.

Manor Farm

It was whilst talking to some of the workforce at Manor Farm that it was noted that long service is, and has been, a strong feature there. At the time of writing (2012), Peter Watts is just completing his 42nd year unbroken, having joined Manor Farm straight from agricultural college. Mike Wing completed 38 years full time and has done 7 years part time

Mick Hockenhull photographed still working aged 90 years

and is still going to the farm daily. But even that record pales alongside the late and well-beloved Mick Hockenhull, who joined Manor Farm under the management of the late Mr. Jack Cook in the 1930s, when Mick was in his 30s. He worked on the farm daily until he was in his 90s, thus completing some 60 years with J. W. Cook and Son.

The Mound

Some two or three centuries ago, there stood, close by the mound, a pair of cottages which were probably toll bar connected. Before the Sherington Bridge establishment and just after the 39/45 War, the road out of Chicheley, known locally as Little End, was re-routed, and during that realignment the footings of the cottages were exposed. This led to a local belief that the area where the mound now stands was a garden for that settlement. That is how the story goes. What is known as fact is that 40 to 50 years ago the area was used by Bucks county council as storage for road chippings. That purpose obtained for a long time until certain 'night-time activities', whatever that may mean, came about, and with it came bottles of drink. The bottles were inevitably smashed and broken in amongst the chippings, thus seriously contaminating the said road dressings. As a result, much of the material had to be condemned; thus the tipping of chippings on that site was discontinued. That then brought the caravan dwellers in and, of course, the untidiness that comes with such. The parish council of Sherington were aware of the complaints made by the residents, justifiably so, and several propositions were submitted, one of which was a drawing (or rather an artist's impression) thought up by a parish councillor, the artwork by a local artist, Caroline Leslie. The scheme got the nod from Sherington councillors and was then passed on to Pat Seymour, our borough councillor at that time (the Liberals being in power). The drawing submitted portrayed a mound 45 feet high with a footpath going round twice, finishing with a seat a top within a balustrade. The second drawing gave an imaginary view across the Ouse Valley from the top of the mound. The borough council recommended it without reserve, and so we saw Messrs. Toby Taylor of Steeple Claydon bring in the spoil and the mound came about – not

Caroline Leslie's drawings of the proposed mound, which were submitted to Buckinghamshire County Council and approved and accepted, 1995

as hoped, but far more than ever expected. Its title was never arranged or proposed, some villager happened to say he had been up the mound and the name stuck. Had it been a little higher, one would have seen clearly into Bedfordshire, but now we must settle for what we have, which is quite acceptable.

Hymn Book Comments

We are told that up until the late 1800s our village church, St. Laud's, was in the see or diocese of Lincoln, thereafter in the diocese of Oxford. At that time one of the churchwardens was Henry George Gardner, who lived and farmed Home Farm in the High Street. Dutifully fulfilling his role as churchwarden, he attended most services. It appears that, betimes, he found the proceedings somewhat tedious, and as a preoccupation would pencil certain comments in his hymn book. He would note that the rector was longwinded in his sermon or one parishioner had a very bad cough etc. Many years later, Henry Gardner's grandson, namely Peter Gardner, aforementioned, was showing the hymn book to a member of the church and, he being a chorister in St. Laud's, started to make notes in his hymn book likewise. This was in the 1970s, 80s and 90s. Some of the observations are listed thus:

Members of Choir – 1978 January

Choir mistress – Mrs. Jill Burgess
Organist – Mrs. F. Jones
Charlotte Smith
Helen Drew
James Cook
Philip Hine
Helen Lanz
Karen Lanz
Anna Cook
Susan Cook
Helen Burgess
Jill Burgess
Victoria Pipes
Elsie Lusted

Joyce Cuffley
Edna White
Mark Hine
Robin Hine
Terence Hine
Noel Gotts
Philip Smith
Rector – Rev. John Corfield

Bellringers – 1978

David Williams, Church End
David Lewis, Gun Lane
Derek Ferris, School Lane
Ella Field, Park Road
Fred Mead, Church Road
John Burgess, Gun Lane
Philip E. Smith, Water Lane

Churchwardens

John Goss
John Furnival

Sherington School Headmistress

Mrs. Kathleen Russell

The following items are not in date order, but just casual shots.

On Monday, March 2nd 1998, fourteen members of Sherington church choir sang a performance of Stainer's Crucifixion in Kings College, Cambridge. There were over 500 voices in the Royal School of Music Choir, to which Sherington belonged, under the resident Musical Director, Stephen Cleobury Esq.

One of the warmest mid-Augusts on record – 1997.

On Tuesday 17th November 2001, Mrs. Betty Feasey of School Lane went to Buckingham Palace to receive the Medal of the British Empire from Her Majesty The Queen.

Four seeds in a hole. One for the rook, one for the crow, one to rot and one to grow.

Charles Stephens, one-time Headmaster at Sherington School, still singing in St. Laud's Choir in his 88th year.

Trevor Findull and his wife Eleanor leave the Swan Inn on 10th March 2003.

A glider crashed near Manor Farm and brought the power lines down. No injuries were sustained. 12th August 2000.

Over 100 communicants at St. Laud's on Easter Day, 1999.

Kelvin Locke Jnr. of the White Hart captained the English under 19s against Sri Lanka. August 2000.

The variety concert in the village hall was completely sold out of tickets for both nights. 12th and 13th December 1980.

Edward Pepper's mother is moving home. She was a 100 years old last August. April 2000.

Wheat prices down to £62 per ton. 1998.

Wheat prices move to £165 per ton. 2007.

On 21st December 1980 at the Christmas service in Sherington church, twenty-nine robed members of the choir were in attendance; all but one, Peter Massingberd Munday, from this Parish.

Oxford won the boat race – Cambridge came second.

Her Royal Highness Princess Margaret worshipped at Astwood church during Advent 1980.

*Whilst Shepherds watched their flocks by night
All seated on the ground
Oh, here's the sidesman coming round
Can you lend me a pound?*

Work on Sherington Bypass abandoned over the New Year 1980 owing to severe frost.

Mr. and Mrs. Alan Cull and family were the first to move into Carters Close on 7th January 1979.

New houses in Carters Close for sale at £18,550.

All roads to Bedford closed because of heavy snow. Many drivers spent the night in Astwood village hall. 15th February 1979.

Mr. Harry Loxley passed from this life on Good Friday 16th April 1981. He was one of the last six men in this village who served in the 1914/18 War. A fine man.

Always get your seed potatoes in by Good Friday.

Virginia House closed for trading. 31st January 2010.

Children's play area next the village hall nearly complete. 16th May 1981.

Over 30 houses in Carters Close complete and occupied. December 1979.

Mr. Jack Cook's dog was seized by the local authority and impounded to the local kennels. He was asked to pay £5 for the release of his canine friend when he demanded its return, but he refused to pay the £5 fine, saying, "The dog must pay that". May 1980.

Two boys tied the church porch doors together during morning service, January 1981. The rector had to go out by the back door to release his flock.

Petrol goes up to £1.60 a gallon and beer is now 52p. a pint.

Our village post office closed permanently. November 2009.

"The ole parson does go on so."

There you have just a few of the comments made and written in a hymn book during morning service over a period of more than 30 years.

C. H. Smith & Sons Ltd

Harry Smith came from Hartwell, Northants well over 90 years ago to cut and clear timber from Sherington Wood, and he stayed on in the

A 1918 Traffic lorry in the livery of C. H. Smith & Sons Ltd.

C. H. Smith & Sons' fleet of 'Big J' Guy lorries

village for the rest of his life. Before leaving Hartwell, Mr. Smith was employed as a horseman by Thomas Basketfield, the local carrier, and found himself able to borrow sufficient money to purchase the business on Mr. Basketfield's retirement.

The name was changed to C. H. Smith, Timber Merchant and Carrier, and much later to C. H. Smith & Sons Ltd. Progressing from horse-drawn carriages to motorised transport in the 1920s enabled him to run a passenger service locally, and later to operate much heavier goods vehicles. The C. H. Smith company employed much local labour, and in the post-war years the company vehicles could be seen anywhere in the United Kingdom.

Over a lifetime, Sherington has been long associated with motor transport, and memory brings to mind: J. T. Burgess, Vincent Pipes, Easyload Transport, C. J. Haynes, and Ken Temple with his mixconcrete vehicle.

Trees

Do you remember a song of yesteryear called, 'Among My Souvenirs', wherein it named so many items of one's life that one has kept, 'just in case'? In case of what is another matter. Amongst the souvenirs to hand, is a small booklet of 36 pages, and was written by the most loyal of Newportonians, namely Peter Adams; always a joy to meet, and his writings were always a joy to read. From that book, entitled *Neath Brooklands Boughs*, we quote the following:

> *Give me the man whose heart is sad, when the woodman fells the tree,*
>
> *For he is the man who understands, just how things have to be.*
>
> *He knows that though the tree must fall, it shall not fall in vain,*
>
> *For in the hands of those who care, the tree will live again.*
>
> *For the tree, a humble servant, to man's incessant need,*

Gives comfort, strength and beauty, to those who pay her heed.

And those who pay her due respect, shall more than profit gain,

As hand and eye appraise the charm, the humble tree can claim.

So give me the man who cares for trees, and the bounties they provide,

For such a man would be my friend, my mentor and my guide.

This village is not without such men. Over a lifetime, many hundreds of trees have been planted, and how important is such an exercise, following that most ruthless of woodland killers, the Dutch elm disease, that laid bare much of our local countryside during the 70s and 80s. This area was rich in elm trees, they being the greatest in number hereabouts. But here we are some 40 years later, well blessed with tree planting. Records show that in February 1981 Mr. Bill Inns, well-remembered employee at Manor Farm, planted 50 chestnut trees along the roadside hedgerow

Planting trees in Stonepits Copse (also known as Stonepit Close), 22nd November 2009

from Manor Corner to Russell Sharpe's turnpike and up the allotment hill. Also recorded is that 2,000 trees were planted within this parish for the millennium. Yet another item says that on 31st March 1981 Dave Williams, Dennis Cheeseman, David Samm and others planted 10 chestnuts and 40 conifers on Perry Lane sports field. It never stopped raining all day. The laurel bushes in the corner of the play area behind the shop were planted on 14th February 1981 – collected from Milton Keynes old village and donated by Fred Mead. In Water Lane stands a Canadian maple in memory of Mrs. Edna White, a much-loved village lady. One or two in memory of Peter Gardner, and a fine walnut in memory of Muriel Cook on Manor Corner. The row of ash trees alongside Gun Lane were planted in the 1980s by Derek Ferris, Dave Williams and others. They were donated by Mr. Ben Crook of Coney Grey. And, of course, there are many small plantations on Manor Farm Estate and Chester Estate, coupled with Water Lane Farm plantations and Top Spinney.

And it must be pointed out that the village's own field, Stonepit Close, in recent years was over-planted with a variety of woodland species that, in the years ahead, will give much pleasure to the parish – 300/400 in number.

Pipelines

It is not generally known in the village of the pipeline that carries a service every minute of every hour throughout the year to other far-reaching destinations. Some 50 years ago there appeared a new source of energy now known as natural gas. Explorers bored beneath the sea bed and transferred the gas to a port on the Thames Estuary, whereby it was piped in land to various destinations, and in our particular interest it was piped from the Thames to Manchester and district, with a branch line within our parish serving Wellingborough and district. Within the curtilage of Sherington parish the pipeline comes over Far Side, crossing the Newport/Bedford road just above Russell Sharpe's farm and on into the gas compound on the Newport side of Manor Farm, whence it travels at the back of Smith's yard, crossing Water Lane 'bout a hundred yards down the private road to End Farm. Thereafter, over the village boundary left of Mare Hill, and onwards past Weston Underwood and Ravenstonc onwards and forwards to the north country. Running alongside that service is another pipeline carrying cement slurry from the Dunstable/Pitstone and Hertfordshire area to Rugby. It feeds the Rugby Portland Cement Company at its plant in that Warwickshire town. Yet another service is a communication service, reckoned to be a telephonic system, but at any rate, a cable of some high importance in that field. At the time all this was going on, there was a suggestion that the Post Office were thinking of yet another pipeline taking the Royal Mail, it being blown through the pipe by air pressure. What truth there was in that idea is not known, but we do remember old Olly saying he would like to dig a hole through the pipe and take out all the registered envelopes!

Final Snippets

In closing, one cannot help but think on the words of wisdom offered by many a village sage …

◊　Mr. Jack Cook was to say that when he announced his move to Mercers Farm in 1931 he was told that, should he behave himself in Sherington, he would do well.

◊　Mr. George Ireland always quoted William Cowper's hymn: "God moves in a mysterious way. Let vengeance on 'em fall."

◊　Jack Pateman, when leaving Stoke Mandeville Eye hospital near Aylesbury, was asked was his sight any better? He replied that he could see Hanslope spire, some thirty miles away.

◊　Ted Adkins, telling us of a low-flying aircraft across his meadow, reckons he looked out of his bedroom window and looked down on the pilot as it flew past, it was so low.

◊　The fisherman who had been down Sherington waters with his rod caught some jellyfish, seven different flavours.

◊   Matty walked from the Chester Arms to Newport Swan in no time at all with three minutes to spare.

◊   Dusty was telling them that the sun always shines on Christmas Day; he had seen it score of times.

◊   Doey, whilst rabbiting with Peter Gardner, said, whilst pointing to the bushes, "I know there's a rabbit in there 'cos I see it come out."

◊   Old Bob, bemoaning the bird nuisance in his garden, "Come and look at my onions, I ain't got one left."

◊   Gran, to the boys climbing the tree, "Don't you fall out that tree and break your leg and come running to me for sympathy."

◊   Old Fred, who went to see Doctor Clay about his health, "Ole Clay put that thing in me mouth and took me template."

George Ireland, with his cup of tea, sitting on the binder next to his daughter Doreen and three of her children

The remarks that have just been read are from the mouths of those with whom we have spent our lives in this small corner of the county of Buckinghamshire, and if, in the time ahead, should anyone be asked about the words and contents of these pages you merely have to reply, "A little bird told me."

Philip E. Smith
Water Lane
Sherington
Buckinghamshire

Floods in Water Lane, 1980s